BREAKING THE CODE

BREAKING THE CODE

An esoteric study:
of numbers and their meanings
of years and their patterns

DONNA LINN

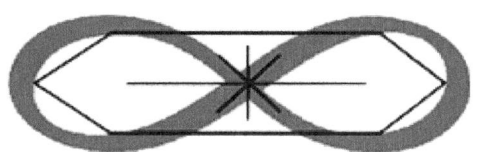

Copyright© 2011 by Donna Linn
Library of Congress Control Number: 2011937841
ISBN:978-0-98450-885-3

All rights reserved. No part of this publication may be reproduced, stored in a retrieval system, or transmitted, in any form or by any means electronic, mechanical, photocopying, recording, or otherwise without prior written permission from the publisher.

The author and publisher of the book do not make any claim or guarantee for any physical, mental, emotional, spiritual, or financial result. All products, services and information provided by the author are for general education and entertainment purposes only. The information provided herein is in no way a substitute for medical or other professional advice. In the event you use any of the information contained in this book for yourself, the author and publisher assume no responsibility for your actions.

Big Country Publishing, LLC accepts no responsibility or liability for any content, bibliographic references, artwork, or works cited contained in this book.

Published by Big Country Publishing, LLC
7691 Shaffer Parkway, Suite C, Littleton, CO 80127
www.bigcountrypublishing.com

Printed in the United States of America
International printing in the U.K. and Australia

TABLE OF CONTENTS

Forward	iii
Acknowledgements	v
Introduction	1
PART 1	
Chapter 1—Exoteric (Basic) Numerology	5
Chapter 2—Esoteric Numerology	7
Chapter 3—Numbers and Their Meanings	13
Chapter 4—The Number Parallelogram	17
Chapter 5—Numbers as Civilizations	25
Chapter 6—Master Numbers	31
Chapter 7—Initiation Numbers	39
Chapter 8—How to Interpret the Chart	45
PART 2	
Chapter 9—Important Years, Part 1	53
Chapter 10—Important Years, Part 2	69
Chapter 11--Years in a Triangle	77
PART 3	
Chapter 12—Time Line Patterns	79
Chapter 13—The Nines Pattern	83
Chapter 14—The Three-Sixes Pattern	91
Chapter 15—The 1-2-4-8-7-5 Pattern	105
Chapter 16—Diamond of Life	139
PART 4	
Chapter 17—Conclusions	147
PART 5	
Addendum	151
Bibliography	159
About The Author	163

ABOUT BREAKING THE CODE

Breaking the Code, Donna Linn's masterwork of numerology transcends all information on the subject that I have encountered. Her work will transform basic numerology which has existed for quite some time into a scientific study with depth akin to astrology. I expect her work to become THE reference book on the subject.

    -Todd Rohlsson, Living Light Alchemy Designs

Breaking the Code is a most amazing book that takes numerology to the next level. I've read many books on numerology, this book is the college edition. I was amazed at the accuracy of the reading with happenings in my life.

    -Matthew Pierce, I. T. consultant

This is the next step. An absolute wealth of information, Breaking the Code is a must-have for any serious numerologist.

    -Tia Adams, artist and energy healing practitioner

Finally, a book that takes Numerology to an advanced level that includes Kabala and Sacred Geometry. Donna has expanded Numerology to a whole new dimension, which expands your client's readings to a much deeper level.

    -Joy Kauf, Owner of Miracles of Joy, Louisville, Tx.

Through this next level of numerology, Donna brings a greater awareness to the reader about themselves, and future life events.

    -Todd Branson, co-author Higher Mind, Lower Mind

So you know Numerology, eh kid? Welcome to the next stage, and beyond.

    -Shannon Adams, hobby numerologist

FORWARD

In 1988, I was still living in Santa Fe, New Mexico, but was traveling around the country lecturing and doing activations. I was the featured speaker at a Gem & Mineral Show in Louisville, Kentucky, speaking on Crystals and Healing when I met Rich and Donna. How any of us connect and find each other is always a story in itself. Someday, I'll share the story of how I came to be in Louisville. It's a really good story, but right now all that is important is that this was where I met Rich and Donna. They asked me to come to their center/store in Northern Kentucky and "teach workshops." I don't so much teach as activate, but maybe that's just semantics. I was also doing private sessions at their center. I have been doing this work a long time in this lifetime and I rarely remember individual sessions. In both Rich and Donna's cases, such extraordinary things unfolded that I do remember things that happened with each of them.

Donna always seemed to feel Rich was the more advanced of the couple. While that assessment is far from true, I totally agree that Rich was pretty darn incredible. They were each unique with a different skill set but they totally complimented and supported each other in a wonderful partnership. During one session with Rich, an ascended Reiki master Dr. Mikao Usui merged with him and Rich, already gifted, was able to go further and do what was intended as the goal of Reiki rather than the entry level energy work that most Reiki practitioners actually do. During a session with Donna, fairies came from all over the planet to take residence at their farm.

Donna had begun writing Breaking the Code before we met. She had also written a book on crystals (another area where we really connect) and her notes on herbs really should be turned into another book. Someone remind her that I'm still nagging about that one. Breaking the Code contains information for an awakening Humanity. Donna is an amazing woman who has never really gotten how truly valuable she is. She spent decades teaching children in the public schools all the while providing a space for people to grow and a platform for others to share their gifts. Each child in every class was important to her just as everyone who came through the center had value to her. She is one of those rare individuals who go unnoticed by the multitude who are so busy looking for glitter that they are blind to the gold. An authentically humble person with talents she does not even know she has, Donna has written an invaluable book that is both channeled and extremely well researched. She has said I have nagged her to get it published and that is most definitely true. I have. And rightly so.

While I've told people about this book and insisted they contact her to get a copy, Donna continued to stay open. She has recently received new information and added that to the already extremely useful information on the language of mathematics and how that helps explain our lives for us thus making this book even more pertinent to everyone. Although a highly intelligent person, she readily admits she's not a mathematician. That did not stop her. She has taken all that was given to her and written it in a way anyone can use. As she says, if she can do the math, anyone (even I) can do it.

There's a certain level of magic in this book as well. Sometimes I read it and immediately "get it." Other days, the words just blur and squiggle on the page. My advice to the reader: do not be deterred. I know she states it's not for everyone, but if the timing is right, it is for anyone interested in authentically going beyond the basics of numerology and who is also willing to do the work.

Read it. Re-read it. And share the knowledge – it all adds up.

Blessings:

Susan Harmon

January 28, 2011

ACKNOWLEDGEMENTS

My life has seen many changes, as everyone does. I wanted answers to greater questions, but I wanted to find them for myself, not depend on others and didn't know where to look. My first husband was teaching college and he "happened" to have in his class two students with whom we became friends. They introduced me to astrology and talked to us endlessly about psychic stuff. They even introduced me to a psychic and a whole world of new concepts and information. I dove into getting the knowledge as fast as I could, with astrology classes and psychic development classes—and any other part of this world that crossed my path. This was while working full time in an era and place where this interest was very much frowned upon and while raising two rambunctious boys involved in all kinds of sports. The marriage couldn't stand the stresses of this time. We grew apart and finally divorced.

My second marriage was to a man totally involved with the psychic world, and especially interested in energy healing. He was a natural healer, and was trying to find modalities that would give his healing ability an outlet that was "acceptable". In our little area of the world, hands-on healing was not looked upon with favor. We learned Reiki, went to different groups, learned many different things and met many wonderful people who became friends in the process.

We later had a farm (I called it a farmette because all we raised were teenagers, dogs and cats!) and while raising my boys and his boys and girls, I started playing with numerology more deeply, although I had dabbled in it before. I wanted to see if we could become a family without the "stepmother" image. I was given hints for the work during a summer vacation from school while the boys worked on cleaning up the farm. The book was about 25 pages long. Nothing I read said anything about most of these numbers I was getting—and I read every numerology book I could buy or have interlibrary loan get for me. Many of these patterns fairly jumped out at me, and when I became stuck, most times Rich could help me find the answer I needed.

By 1988, the teenagers had gone to college, jobs, etc., and not at home any more. We were very involved with the Cincinnati/Northern Kentucky psychic circle and decided to wholesale crystals and other healing stones. We went to Louisville to a gem show and met Susan. The next year we started a metaphysical center/store and invited her to come to do workshops and crystal healings at our store. She suggested (very strongly, I might add) that I work on my book and try to get it published. By 1997, I had done this and had found even more numbers that interested me. I did a few readings and they seemed to resonate with other people. So I rewrote the small book, turned it into about 100 pages, sent it for copywrite, and wrote a few publishers that I thought might be interested. Everyone refused it, so it sat on the shelf. I sold some of those copies through word of mouth (especially Susan and our store) but did not actively market it. She pushed me for years to get this book published and out into the world, but when it didn't move, I learned about herbs, ran the store with Rich and all that entails, and forgot about it for several years.

Rich died. I moved to Texas and started playing with the numbers again, looking in my chart and a friend's chart for specific dates. We couldn't find what we wanted, so I kept looking and found a major hole in the numbers I had been using. I even found that the time and place of birth is important in your numbers, not just the date of birth!

When I came to Texas, I needed to find a store with like-minded people, because no one around me was involved with things of the spirit. I finally found a store (took me two months), and I started going to classes and psychics that came into the store. I was looking for my next life step, because everything had closed up and I was hunting for a door to step into. These psychics did not know anything about me (and some didn't know each other), but they all told me the same thing! Get the book finished and published. (They did not know I had this book pretty well done). One gave me a deadline of February, another made me promise to have it finished in January, 2011. (I kept saying the END of January.) So I guess now is the time for this book to finally get published, and out into the world.

This book is not for everyone. Many will pick it up. There are parts in the esoteric area that will seem strange and the year numbers are difficult to follow at first because of the pagination. Just keep in mind there are only five stems and they do not change indiscriminately. There is the nine, the three/six, and three of the 1, 2, 4, 8, 7, 5 stems. This is consistent from year one to year 4000. Every year that I use in 1900-2050 has these stems, and the way to get them involves some mathematical skill (which I don't have!). But if I can do it, anyone can do it—if they take the time to figure it out. I have made it as simple as I could—for myself and for you.

This is my own interpretation of the numbers. I use one or two words for each number and then show how they work together for larger numbers (I go up to 999). Using all the letters A=1 to Z=26, you can find higher master numbers, initiation numbers (for self and soul). Numerology is not just for your life now—it is to show you your soul lessons so that you can help your soul grow more easily, in addition to the usual numbers for your life in the physical realm.

In finding these numbers, I looked for patterns and many just jumped out at me. Math is not my strong suit, so the math part was hard, especially using all the stems which give you an idea of what the next years will bring.

There is not a family group in this book because of the sensitive nature of this information. No family, including my own, was willing to have their numbers put into a published account for everyone to see their lessons to learn.

I am cognizant that everyone who put my feet on this path of self-development was playing their role in this book. There are too many to name, but they come from all walks of life, and interests. I will be forever grateful for those beings who set me on this path, knowingly or unknowingly. For many times, it was just in conversation that something said set me on the quest for more information. Then I would sit down and just "know" what I was looking at. The ideas were given to me through books, people, unknown beings. The hardest part was then putting it in words.

Those who have been most instrumental in my growth are as follows, but this is by no means exclusive.

Sandy and Jeff, who introduced me to the fascinating inner worlds and ways to access them

Ginny and Ed, who gave me access to books on all "new age" and "old" information and led me further into these new worlds.

Joyce, who was an early mentor and friend

Librarians at Campbell County Library, Cold Spring branch, who introduced me to interlibrary loan and helped find many obtuse works

Deborah, who was there when I needed someone to talk to about these inner subjects and many other subjects.

Susan, who was much more than a workshop presenter, but also has been a friend and mentor all these many years.

Joy, Matthew, Shannon, Malachite, and the rest of the group of new friends who focused me on my next path and gave me the courage to accept it.

Christina and her graphic artists, for their works of magic on this book.

Tia, who showed me all the ways computers can play with drawings.

Rich, who was my partner, my friend, and my supporter in everything I chose to do. To all the unknown (to me) inner beings who helped in this work, I give my great gratitude, yet for any mistakes in interpretation, I take full responsibility.

It has been an eventful life, and for all the difficulties that come with the territory, I have enjoyed learning all the many ways self-development happens, and all the different paths it can take. There is a path for every interest and preference!

INTRODUCTION

Numerology has always been one of the least known and least used of the psychic sciences. It has had many proponents who were famous, such as those authors whose books are listed in the bibliography. E.S.P., astrology, even Tarot have had many more adherents.

Numerology seems to be too easy. There are only nine numerals and zero. How can you use only these numerals and know so much about an individual when all persons are unique? Can these numerals be at all accurate for a person? Answers to these questions can only come from using the numbers and deciding for yourself. Keep an open mind and when you don't see any connections at once, stop and think about how you react to situations, to other people. Perhaps the number is showing you how to act differently in a situation, or what would be an easier way for you.

We are all creatures of habit and learning. Many times the paths we choose for certain situations in our life are the hardest, the most circuitous. Numerology can show strengths you might not know you have. It can make you aware of certain stressful years and the pattern within your changing life.

The only thing certain about life is that it changes! How you accept and flow with change, how you cooperate with this change (good OR bad, in your eyes) will decide which of the lessons chosen will be learned and which will be left to another time. Numerology can make you aware of these major changes within your life and the pattern emerging for your life lessons.

Much has been written on the numerology of the exoteric (I call it basic numerology). This includes the numbers one through nine and all the meanings found for those numbers. Many excellent books have been written elucidating what each number of your name means in each position within the chart.

This book focuses on the esoteric or hidden meanings of the expanded numbers and the energy within those numbers that shows up only as the negative of a photograph. We can only have a photograph if it has been snapped on a film and developed. Our life is much like that. Outside we have the photograph that is shown to the world, but inside we must have the film to process into that photograph. The photograph is the exoteric part of numerology, while the esoteric part of numerology is like the film BEFORE being processed. It can also be looked at as a ball—the outside is the you you see and the inside that has air in it is the soul. Both numbers together show what we have learned and what we need to process in our life now. It is the design of our life, the structure of the building, the foundation upon which we are building.

Knowing about our numbers in an esoteric way, we can accommodate to our learning more easily, moving WITH the flow of life instead of AGAINST it.

I believe numbers have two meanings within the esoteric meaning. The number you see AND its complement (1-9, 2-8, 3-7, 4-6, 5 alone). Each has a special way of being read for meaning. Then there are "initiation" numbers and "master" numbers. There are numbers for each of nine civilizations that we have had or will have for our earth lessons. There are numbers for old and new energy patterns, transition numbers, numbers for end-of-cycle lives. The numbers also account for the people with whom you work and play. Each grouping you belong to is a specific group designed for learning and/or recreating a specific karmic situation—all individuals brought together for a detailed purpose and when that purpose has been accomplished, that specific group will be disbanded. Sometimes the total group will disintegrate, other times certain individuals will leave and new persons enter.

Family groups are especially fun to play with because the numbers can tell from which civilization they are experiencing common lessons, to which parent (if not both) the child (or children) belongs, which lesson (or lessons) the family is learning—and it will be a group lesson—why they chose to come into incarnation as a group and why at this time. There are certain numbers in certain places that will be the same for the whole family (even step-families)—a fascinating look at the web we weave in order to return to the One with our lessons learned.

One can read the change in lessons for the woman when she changes her name by marriage and takes on her husband's last name—or even hyphenates it to her own. Because most women at the time of marriage take the husband's last name, they have more "opportunity"—more lessons to learn, more opportunities to grow and change in our society than the man. It seems to be becoming a matriarchal society and the woman must become much more the bearer of light—the beacon holder, while the man must help uphold and uplift that light. Changing her name through marriage gives the woman more numbers to work through, but also more opportunities to grow and develop the qualities needed to bring that light into the world at this time.

Each person has a unique place in the universe. It is his (or hers) and his (or hers) alone. NO ONE else can fill that particular spot in the design of the universe. Numerology can help one to understand where that place is and how to cooperate with his (or her) numbers to grow the most during this time of incarnation. If one knows, then he (or she) is responsible for becoming aware of that place and consciously working toward filling that place and learning the lessons needed for becoming even more of a light-bearer. There are many paths—numerology is only one—for finding that place. But you will find that numerology will complement the other paths and perhaps show you new insight into this game we play called LIFE.

The game of life is an illusion, but the players are real. One of the ways to find out the rules of the game is numerology. The players are those people with whom you are in contact each day. How you react toward each of them can be seen within the numbers of your name and theirs. And sometimes you can even re-enact a previous situation and change the result! The numbers in the following chapters will explain how you too can break the code, can find the hidden knowledge that is in the numbers of your own unique name and birthday. It is not quite as easy as exoteric numerology, but much more in depth about your life.

If your numbers indicate a readiness for change, it WILL happen and cannot be blocked. It may not be in the conscious, but within the subconscious, or the supra-conscious. How you react to the change that happens indicates how much of that lesson has been learned—and how well. Life is the way that inner plane lessons are practice, learned, and applied—by the outer self!

The ideas in this book are not mine, but I have attempted to apply them in a different and perhaps more expansive way. When I needed an outlet for fun and new knowledge, "they" put my feet on this path. I can only hope that your entry into this path will be as interesting and productive as mine has been. Have fun learning more about yourself and the years that are important to you in the following pages. I have had fun and learned much that I have not found in any other of the psychic areas.

Donna Linn

March, 1997, January, 2011

Chapter 1

EXOTERIC (BASIC) NUMEROLOGY

Changing the letters of your name to numbers, as well as adding the numbers of your birthdate is called Numerology. It is a mathematical way to encode knowledge of purpose, of lessons, of talents, making it accessible to anyone who knows the key. This has been used for many, many years—even back before Hebraic times, perhaps even to Atlantis or before to learn about a person. Numerology, as an aid to learning life's lessons, has not been used nearly as much in recent times as, for instance, astrology, palmistry and tarot have been. If we understand how, we can read the code that can tell us all the things we need to know about ourselves and how to go more easily through life's lessons.

The numbers in your name and birthdate are uniquely yours. No one else has exactly the same heritage as yours—even those who are identical twins (different names). You are a unique combination of what has happened before and what you have left to experience. For every deed—both good and bad—that you have done and had done to you, a balance must be struck before the karma of that life can be finished. Many times it cannot be finished in one lifetime, and so both you and the other person come back, together or separately, in a different setting to finish the lesson. If you learn the lesson, your part is finished.

A short review of exoteric numerology is in order. In this numerology, the only numbers used are single digit. Whenever you have double digit numbers, each digit is added together until a single digit number is obtained.

The only exceptions are double numbers 11, 22, and 33, which are considered master numbers. Any book in numerology will give you many meanings for each single digit number. They are accurate, but limited.

In basic numerology, each letter is given a one digit numeral to be added together in order to find a total number for your name and birthdate.

1	2	3	4	5	6	7	8	9
A	B	C	D	E	F	G	H	I
J	K	L	M	N	O	P	Q	R
S	T	U	V	W	X	Y	Z	

These are the basic numerology codes. In the numerology which we have used for many years, the numbers tell us about the lessons to be experienced in this lifetime and how we may react to each different situation.

Using my name, Donna, in basic numerology, we find D=4, O=6, N=5, N=5, A=1 for a total of 4+6+5+5+1=21, reduced to 3 (1+2). Another name (in basic numerology), Jonathan) would be J=1, O=6, N=5, A=1, T=2, H=8, A=1, N=5 for a total of 1+6+5+1+2+8+1+5=29/11 (not reduced to 2 because it is a master number).

The birthdate would also be made into numbers –the month in sequence, January=1, December =12=3 (written 12/3); the days 1 and 10 both equal 1; 2, 20=2, 11 (not reduced because it is a master number); 3, 12, 21 all = 3; 4, 13, 31 equal 4 and so on. The year is added together—1994=1+9+9+4=23/5. A birthdate of February 7, 1978 would be February (2), 1978 (1+9+7+8+=25/7) which becomes 2+7+7=16/7.

Chapter 2
ESOTERIC NUMEROLOGY

The majority of people are not interested in numerology or think of it as the work of the devil! How can nine numbers tell you anything about yourself? By reading this far, you have placed yourself within the 10% of people interested either in numerology or in new ideas. NO ONE will pick up and read this book accidentally, though it might seem so at the time. Many of the ideas herein are not new, but I have not found much of this in print, and many people seem to be interested in some of this "new" old material. Some books on numerology have one or two sentences on one or two parts of this work. And some of it I have not seen anywhere in my searches. The mystery schools of ancient times knew all we know and much, much more that has been lost. As we have been told, all hidden knowledge will become plain. It is my feeling that this material is part of that plan. Many practitioners of numerology need to read and comment upon the validity of this material for themselves. I use it, and believe this work is valid.

Much writing exists on the numerology of the exoteric. What I am talking about in this book is another way to use numbers to understand the inner you, perhaps even the soul lessons that you came to learn. I have given it the name of Esoteric Numerology, because most of the information I was given seems to have been hidden for an age. At one time, it was probably used very much like the astrology in Tibet to find out what was going to happen in a child's lifetime. This work focuses on the esoteric or hidden meanings of numbers and the energy within that shows only as a photograph with its negative. We must have the negative of the photograph (soul) in order to get a picture (physical body) to show the outer world. The esoteric part of numerology is like the film being processed. It shows what we have learned and what we need to process in our life now. Esoteric numerology is a matter of working with the inner meanings of the many numbers and combinations of numbers within your name and birth date. That name and birth date is an amalgamation of many paths, many incarnations of learning, and much help from other people both within physical life and non-physical life to become the unique person that each of us is. It was given so that we may experience the lessons of this life and lifetime, and remember what we have already learned.

I believe numbers function as a template, or mold, to show past experiences, present potentials, and what—if anything—will be left to a future time. It is as if the soul, when it decided to come back to earth-living again, decides what lessons it needs to learn, what situations need to be met to fulfill karmic debts and makes a beginning pattern that will aid it in this lifetime. That is coded in what becomes your name at birth. Many times that name only lasts two or three days before it is shortened, or the child is given a nickname. How many times has a new-born child not used his/her birth certificate name until much later—or even the name chosen before birth changed when he/she was named after arriving in this lifetime. This is because the name chosen before birth does not correspond with what the baby needs to learn in this precise incarnation. The child uses this name until such time that he/she chooses a new name. Most children during school years will play with a changed name—Katherine/Kay/Kathy/Kate/Katie, or Edward/Eddie/Ed (or back to the original name shortened since birth). This new name encodes those new numbers which show other lessons to be learned this lifetime. The first name is used only until the karma and lessons are finished.

The numbers of the new name then take precedence in what needs to be learned. This continues with any new name taken—there will be new lessons, new learnings, new situations, new talents encountered, as these numbers are added to the birth name, even though the birth numbers underlie the new numbers.

The birth date is one of the key elements in numerology. How many babies are born on their due date? I believe that each soul who comes into this world already knows what it will experience during this lifetime, be it short or long, and what date on which to arrive in order to accomplish those lessons. This, to me, is why some children come earlier or later than they are "expected".

My way of looking at numerology is to give each letter the value of its place in the alphabet: A=1, K=11, Z=26. This gives you the same basic number, but with many more variations within the name. For instance, E=5, N=14, W=23. All can reduce to five, but the N and W give nuances of the original number 5. The E as five is change, the N as 14 uses a one (self) and 4 (foundations) to work with change, while the W uses a two (balance) and three (associations) to describe the change. Therefore each letter—even though it reduces to the same number (E, N, W=5)--works through different vibrations towards the same end.

By using A=1 to Z=26, one has the ability to discriminate more closely between different meanings of the same basic number and to become more specific about any individual person. Each number for J to Z uses nuances to work through the general definitions of the reduced number. But it also gives a totally different name number and birth number, although it will reduce to the same number as exoteric numerology. The number "1" may also be 10, 19, 28, 37, 46, 55. Each has a different emphasis which gives a more closely individualistic approach to a numerology reading.

When using the expanded numerology, the following chart will be helpful for labeling the letters:

A=1 B=2 C=3 D=4 E=5 F=6 G=7 H=8 I=9
J=10 K=11 L=12 M=13 N=14 O=15 P=16 Q=17 R=18
S=19 T=20 U=21 V=22 W=23 X=24 Y=25 Z=26

Let's use these names again to explain how the numbers work: D=4, O=15, N=14, N=14, A=1. The name "Donna" adds up to 48 (4+15+14+14+1). Do not reduce to 12/3, except to check the math. The name Jonathan adds up to 83 (10+15+14+1+20+8+1+14). Do not reduce to 11, but be aware of it.

This also applies to the birth date. Let's take December 15, 1985. The month stays in order and expanded (December=12), the day stays expanded 15=15, but the year is still reduced to double digits (1985=1+9+8+5=23). Do not reduce any further. The only reason to reduce to single digits is to check the math—December 12/3, day 15/6, and year 23/5. Three + six + five =14/5 which is the same as 50/5.

Five numbers that generally have been important to numerology are the following:

1. Life Number— birth date.
2. Soul Number--adding the vowels in the name
3. Outer Personality Number—adding consonants in the name
4. Destiny Number—total of the Soul plus Outer Personality numbers
5. Power Number—total of Destiny plus Life

I added two more numbers that I have found to be important:

6. Psychic Self—Consonants minus vowels
7. Center or Core Self—Destiny minus Life

The way of using these numbers is exactly the same in basic and expanded numerology, just the number read is different, although the numbers with both reduce to the same single digit. This becomes a check on the accuracy of math.

I always do a name both ways so that I know my math is accurate. Both ways are equally valid and show important aspects of an individual's life and make up, but the esoteric adds information not otherwise obtainable through the numbers.

Breaking the Code 9

Using my name (Donna), we will set up the chart to find out what information we can—using both exoteric (single digit) and esoteric (A-Z=1-26) numbers.

```
        15              1                       =16/7        Soul #
         6              1       =7
D        O    N    N    A       =21/3           =48/12/3    Destiny #
4             5    5            =14/5
4            14   14                            =32/5       Outer Personality #
```

Using my name DONNA, in exoteric numerology, we find that the soul number (vowels) is 7 (6+1), the outer personality (consonants) is 5 (4+5+5=14/5, and the destiny number (total consonants + vowel—7+5) is 12/3. Using the expanded esoteric style, the soul number is 16 (15+1) reduced to 7 and the outer personality number is 32 (4+14+14) reduced to 5, with the destiny number of 16+32=48/12/3, but using the 48 for reference. The 12/3 double checks the single digit of the same number.

Therefore, in basic exoteric numerology the seven as a soul number would mean a name with the possibility of spiritual awareness and understandings. The sixteen in esoteric numerology would mean spiritual awareness (the seven) using the one of leadership and the six of service and responsibility. In the same way, one would read the outer personality and destiny numbers.

Going even further with our esoteric understanding, we will look at the inner numbers. These are regular numbers subtracted from 10 or 100. This shows the film negative number for Soul on the outer plane (exoterically) as 10-7= 3 of associations and on the inner plane (esoterically 100-16=84) building spiritual and physical foundations. The outer personality number exoterically is 5 which means lots of physical changes as is the inner number (esoterically), while the outer personality (esoterically) on the outer plane is 32 giving associations and balance within the change lessons. The outer personality esoterically on the inner plane is 68 with meanings of service and spiritual/business power. The total name (outer number exoterically) is 12/3 showing an affinity for associations and (outer number esoterically) 16+32=48, meaning associations through the nuances of building foundations and power, both physical and spiritual. The film negative for the total name (exoteric) is 7 for spiritual awareness and (esoteric) 52 meaning change, while working through balance and duality. This is explained more fully later on.

Let's do the same thing with a birth date:

Exoteric   9   22   1+9+4+1=15/6   9+22+6=37/10/1

September 22, 1941

Esoteric   9   22   1+9+4+1=15/6   9+22+15=46/10/1

Observe that 37/10/1 and 46/10/1 reduce to the same one. Do not reduce any 11 or 22 found in the day, month, or year in the exoteric number (i.e., the day of the month [22]).

Using the birth date to find out the life path, we use the one (exoteric) to explain the pathway chosen for lessons in this lifetime. A number one chosen for this life contains elements of leadership and self-knowledge and no matter what else the name shows, the person will have opportunities to lead others and learn knowledge about Self. The 46 is also a "one", but shows that the leadership will be through building solid foundations while using service and responsibility.

The film negative of this birth date number one is nine. This number shows that an inner cycle is ending. The 46 (esoteric birth date) negative is 54 which shows that the ending cycle will be through much change and the creation of a solid base.

In summary: Donna

	exoteric	soul film negative	esoteric	soul film negative
Soul	7	3	16	84
Total	12/3	7	48	52
Outer Pers.	14/5	5	32	68
Sept. 22, 1941	37/10/1	9	46/10/1	54

Pay attention to all the numbers that repeat within this name, especially the eights, fours, and sixes.

Knowing about our numbers in an esoteric way, we can accommodate to our learning more easily, because we have more information to use. With this system, we can understand why and how some of the patterns in our life have happened—and how we can learn from and let go of these particular patterns of our life.

Breaking the Code 11

There is much in this chapter that will be more elaborately explained later on in these pages, but this chapter contains a brief summary of some—not nearly all—of the information that can be gleaned by using all 26 letters in our alphabet--not just the nine single digits--and by using the film negative numbers. I'm sure there is even more that I have not written about that can be learned using the full numbers instead of nine digits.

Chapter 3
NUMBERS AND THEIR MEANINGS

Any numerology book will give you meanings of the numbers one through nine, usually several paragraphs-worth of meanings and nuances, and variations of meanings. I have taken very basic meanings and have tried to show how different numbers that reduce to the same single digit use those variations of meanings to actually apply to the larger number. Using the original number broadens the meaning of the single digit number and tells by what means the single digit number may be learned. These lessons can be on any of three levels—subconscious, conscious, or supra-conscious. Consider the numbers as steps on a ladder. I have chosen to use only one or two words for each meaning to simplify the new way of handling the more numbers used with my esoteric numerology.

Those people working on the lessons of self and leadership in this world have the key number one. It includes 10, 19, 28, 37, 46, 55, 64, 73, 82, and 91. Every number has a double single digit within its sequence of numbers that has other important considerations in addition to this set and which will be taken up in another chapter. Many people at this time are learning leadership and self-knowledge. There are many, many groups each needing a leader—from family and extended family, small interest groups, organized groups, even to and through national and international groups. Everyone within the "one" path will be learning about themselves through leadership roles whether large groups or small.

The challenge of the number two is that of duality, balance, and harmony. Duality is more than dealing with two sides of an issue. It includes the ability to find balance and harmony in all things. The numbers on this rung of the ladder are 11, 20, 29, 38, 47, 56, 65, 74, 83, and 92. At some place in the number profile most people will find this lesson. I think of the twos as using a scale and trying to keep both sides level--whether it is family and work, social and quiet time, or any other type of balancing act to find harmony and equilibrium.

Cooperation, communication, and associations belong to all people with the numbers of three. The numbers include: 12, 21, 30, 39, 48, 57, 66, 75, 84, and 93, Again, each single digit three has different lessons, but all are played out while communicating on the stage of cooperation and association.

Those with four—13, 22, 31, 40, 49, 58, 67, 76, 85, and 94—are working on shades of building solid foundations, creations and physical power. As with all the other numbers, these can show up in the subconscious, conscious, and supra-conscious.

Change, freedom, and adaptability are the next rung on our ladder. The fives: 14, 23, 32, 41, 50, 59, 68, 77, 86, and 95 all deal with change and flexibility. It is the same on both the physical and spiritual planes. Both inner and outer planes resonate to the number five. Thus, consider five as a pivot number. With a five, flexibility is the lesson—inner and outer!

Sixes include the numbers 15, 24, 33, 42, 51, 60, 69, 78, 87, and 96. These numbers involve service and responsibility. This may be at home, in school, at work, with family, with friends. Sometimes it is in a group situation, sometimes not, but always with an eye toward service and always taking responsibility—even if not their own.

The sevens: 16, 25, 34, 43, 52, 61, 70, 79, 88, and 97 are in the process of spiritual awareness and spiritual understanding within this lifetime. You will find them in all religions of the world—traditional and non-traditional—maybe even starting their own. Even if not in an organized religion, they will be searching for a higher purpose.

Eights: 17, 26, 35, 44, 53, 62, 71, 80, 89, and 98 are working on spiritual authority or power and building spiritual bases. These are the business people with responsibility for managing other employees. They will profit only to the extent that they use that power on a spiritual base—treating everyone fairly, etc. If not, beware of the problems yet to be.

The nines: 18, 27, 36, 45, 54, 63, 72, 81, 90, and 99 are end-of-cycle numbers—with 99 being a strong coordination point for jumping to the higher numbers. They are the final chance to use these nuances wisely, cleaning up and clearing out any loose ends shown by these numbers.

In the number sequence of your name, you may find the number series 91 through 99 or the 100 through 109. The 91-99 series can be understood as endings within this lifetime—sort of a test to be sure you have fulfilled the mastery requirements to go on to another learning—the one of self, the two of balance, etc. The 100-109 numbers are the beginnings of a new cycle of learning about that number. They seem to be karmic. At some point during your lifetime, this number will activate, perhaps in a very mundane way, a very small decision made, or a major occurrence. This may also be subconscious, conscious, or supra-conscious.

Chapter 4

THE NUMBER PARALLELOGRAM

I believe the numbers from one to ninety-nine encompass all the basic lessons humanity has to learn. The numbers that reduce to the single digit are only BASIC lessons and comprise the PHYSICAL side of the following table. Any double digit number that when added becomes another double digit number (93=9+3=12=1+2=3) is on the SPIRITUAL side of the table. Each number from 1 to 99 is important within its own right as nuances of the major number, and different aspects of the main number. This is why each number from one to nine can mean many different things. A person with a 46 will not have exactly the same lessons as a person with the number 28 or 37 even though they all reduce to one. Each will be experiencing the necessary work on his/her leadership roles.

Spiritual Numbers   Physical Numbers

91 82 73 64 55 46 37 28 19 10/1\10
    92 83 74 65 56 47 38 29 11/2\11 20
        93 84 75 66 57 48 39 12/3\12 21 30
            94 85 76 67 58 49 13/4\13 22 31 40
                95 86 77 68 59 14/5\14 23 32 41 50
                    96 87 78 69 15/6\15 24 33 42 51 60
                        97 88 79 16/7\16 25 34 43 52 61 70
                            98 89 17/8\17 26 35 44 53 62 71 80
                                99 18/9\18 27 36 45 54 63 72 81 90

The numbers 10-18 can reduce to the number one to 9, but they offer a higher level meaning in the Esoteric System. Each of the digits in a higher decade number shows a part of the emphasis of its meaning within the number to which it reduces. The numbers 10-18 can be either physical or spiritual as noted by being on both sides of the single digit. Any of the eights are numbers of choice, a transition time, while the nines are an age of tremendous growth and the completion of a cycle with the beginning of a new cycle ready to commence. The zeros are the beginning of another level (neither higher nor lower -- just different).

The numbers 10-18 are bridging numbers that allow one to flow between both the physical and spiritual areas of life. If the original number can not be reduced (that is, it becomes one digit), you are on the physical side, i.e. 16/7, 45/9, 24/6 etc. If it can be reduced, 56/11/2, 87/15/6, 64/10/1, etc., then you are using the spiritual side of the chart. The actual meaning of the number is based on the individual's chart and the other numbers that are present. One must consider both possibilities for these numbers and see where they are actually present.

This parallelogram of numbers divides into two triangles, one of which is physical and the other which is spiritual. Not including the single digits one through nine, each triangle has 45 spiritual and 45 physical lessons that we must learn and apply before we can go on to the higher numbers. These lessons include 20 spiritual lessons (opposite numbers—for example 64 and 46), 5 spiritual mastery lessons (55-99) and 16 physical lessons (opposite numbers 14 and 41), 4 physical mastery lessons (11-44), plus nine beginnings (1-9). Each number has its opposite. Opposites are numbers that have the same meaning but are numerically reversed (19-91, 74-47, 28-82). Excluding those of double digit same number, these numbers share the same lesson regardless of which number is in which column, just the weight of the lessons differ. That is, 12 and 21 have the same lesson, as does 49 and 94. The physical side of the triangle is learning the lesson; the spiritual side is applying the knowledge learned from the physical side. These lessons do not include the basic numbers one through nine that are used in Basic Numerology.

Each number also has a complement. Complements are numbers that are left after subtracting the number from 10, 100, or 1000. The complement is the inner plane, or soul, lesson working itself out within our incarnation. What we see is the outer shell of what is really happening. It is as if one is inside a ball of clay and trying to make that ball perfectly round. Each push from inside the ball shows up on the outside surface. So if, on the soul level, one is working on the number one, it will show up on the outside as a nine. The number three shows up as a seven, the four as a six. The number five is the same on both planes. That which we see on the outside is a physical manifestation of the number lesson. As we subtract from 10, 100, 1000, we see lessons manifested, or reasons for experiences of which we are not consciously aware. The same is true of whichever number you are reading—life number, soul number, outer personality number, destiny number, power number, psychic number, center- self number.

18 *Donna Linn*

Each number takes its major characteristic from the single digit number in basic numerology. Then we use the separate individual parts of the main number to find the interpretation. An example is 47, which becomes 11, then 2, perceived to mean the four of foundations plus the seven of spirituality to develop through the master number eleven (two ones for self-knowledge) and the two of duality and balance. Another example is 38: 3+8=11/2—the three of association plus the eight of spiritual power developing lessons through the master number eleven and the two of duality.

The numbers that do not reduce also have lessons, this time more important within the physical sector of our incarnation. 1, 2, 3, 4—mostly seem to be finished, while many people seem to be working on 5, 6, 7, and 8. The nines are mostly physical endings or final tests of learning. They include:

Self and leadership—1, 10
Duality and balance—2, 11, 20
Communication and association—3, 12, 21, 30
Physical Foundations—4, 13, 22, 31, 40
Change and adaptability—5, 14, 23, 32, 41, 50
Service and responsibility—6, 15, 24, 33, 42, 51, 60
Spiritual awareness and understanding—7, 16, 25, 34, 43, 52, 61, 70
Spiritual and physical power—8, 17, 26, 35, 44, 53, 62, 71, 80
Endings—9, 18, 27, 36, 45, 54, 63, 72, 81, 90

Notice that each number has one more lesson than the previous number, that is, one has two physical lessons up to the nines that have 10 physical lessons.

My interpretation of the physical numbers and their lessons are as follows:

2/11—master number 11, learning the use balance and duality

3/12/21—group learning and cooperation

4/13/31—master number 22--building physical foundations

5/14/41, 23/32—learning through many physical changes, in home, work, other places, etc., the need to learn flexibility and adaptability

6/15/51, 24/42, 33—master number 33—learning to be in service to other people

7/16/61, 25/52, 34/43—beginning to work through spiritual involvement—but not necessarily formal religion; this seems to be a very important within this time of earth learning.

Breaking the Code

8/17/71, 26/62, 35/53, 44—master number 44—physical power while learning to use spiritual power—in business, etc., important in the physical world at this time.

9/18/81, 27/72, 36/63, 45/54—ending of physical series indicated by combinations of digits. Many people have these numbers now. It is as if many of us are choosing to finish this particular cycle of earth living.

All the numbers that end with zero are new beginnings, with concentration of focus on the other digit. It is also an opportunity to contact other dimensions more easily.

Ten is the beginning of leadership, while all the other one numbers are spiritual. It is the beginning cycle of self—to learn selfhood and leadership.

Twenty is the beginning cycle of duality—to learn and use duality and balance, while the mastery number 11 is learning balance through self-understanding and leadership potentials.

Thirty is the beginning cycle of association, group learning—to learn cooperation and communication, while 12 and 21 are learning that same lesson through self-understanding and balance. It seems this mostly has been learned on the physical level.

Forty is the beginning cycle of building physical foundations—to reach a higher order of balance as preparation for future learning. 13 and 31 are learning how to use physical power through self and associations. The 22, a master number, is learning how to use power by understanding duality and balance. This also seems mostly learned.

Fifty is learning through many physical changes to understand adaptability and flexibility. The 14/41 is learning to adapt through leadership, physical power and creativity, while the 23/32s are learning to adapt through balance and associations.

Sixty is the beginning of a cycle of service to other people and of responsibility. The 15/51 numbers are learning responsibility through leadership and change. The 24/42s are learning responsibility through balance and physical power, while the master number 33 is learning service through association and cooperation with people and groups—large and small.

Seventy is the gateway for spiritual awareness and understanding. This number is beginning to work toward spiritual involvement—but not necessarily churches. 16/61 is learning about spiritual nature through leadership and service, 25/52 through balance and change, 34/43 through associations and foundational buildings. There are many people here with these numbers. It is a physical learning for spiritual awareness to take place, and very important within this time period of earth learning.

Eighty is the beginning of the cycle of spiritual power, rebirth, teaching about power, and how to use authority in the proper manner. It usually includes physical power, in business, etc. 17/71 is learning to use spiritual power through leadership of a spiritual nature. 26/62 is acquiring knowledge of how to use spiritual power through balance and service while 35/53 is learning through groups and flexibility toward change. The master number 44 is learning how to use spiritual power through physical power and physical creation. These numbers show why business has become very popular as a career path. The eight is a physical number to learn about spiritual power. It is very important in the physical world at this time.

Ninety is the beginning cycle of endings of the physical series indicated by the combination of digits, to teach about humanity and evolution. 18/81 is the end of the cycle of self and ambition, 27/72 is the end of the cycle of balance and spiritual awareness, 36/63 is the end of the cycle of associations and service. 45/54 is the end of the cycle of change and physical power. Many people have these numbers now. It is as if many of us are choosing to finish this physical cycle of earth learning. The nines are completing their growth within the spheres of influence of the two parts of the number.

The spiritual numbers are using those previous physical learnings. This time we have to USE the knowledge that we learned.

Self and leadership—91 82 73 64 55 46 37 28 19
Duality and balance—92 83 74 65 56 47 38 29
Communication and association—93 84 75 66 57 48 39
Physical foundations—94 85 76 67 58 49
Change and adaptability—95 86 77 68
Service and responsibility—96 87 78 69
Spiritual awareness and understanding—97 88 79
Spiritual/physical power—98 89
Endings—99

Notice that self has 91/19, 82/28, 73/37, 64/46, and master number 55 or five lessons. Duality has 92/29, 83/38, 74/47, 65/56, or four lessons. Association has 93/39, 84/48, 75/57, and master number 66 which is four lessons. Physical foundations include 94/49, 85/58, 76/67 or three lessons. Change and adaptability have two lessons-- 95/59, 86/68, plus master number 77. Service has only two lessons--96/69 and 87/78. Power has only one reversible number 98/89, and endings has only one—the master number 99. All of the series 90-99 are end of series reviews of the lessons learned and applied during this life.

Breaking the Code

My interpretation of these lessons is as follows:

Those numbers that reduce to ten are learning self-awareness and leadership. Leadership is spiritual: 91/19, 82/28, 73/37, 64/46, and master number 55.

The 11/2s learn the difference between inner and outer planes. These numbers include 91/19, 83/38, 74/47, 65/56. They are beginning to use spirituality in the outer world. This is happening very much at this time. The twos are here to learn to use balance, but in a spiritual way. These numbers always reduce to the master number 11 before the two.

The 12/3 is the bridge to higher levels of cooperation and a different way of association. These numbers include 93/39, 84/48, 75/57, and master number 66. This different way depends on the combination that makes up 12. The 66 is bringing much responsibility in any group endeavor. Many people have these numbers somewhere in their chart.

The 13/4 is building a bridge from physical foundations to firm foundations in the spiritual realm. These numbers are 94/49, 85/58, 76/67, and are very important in the new paradigm of the world at this time.

The 14/5 is learning how to use change creatively and constructively. These numbers are 95/59, 86/68, and master number 77. This is a difficult lesson. It will take much time to learn all the facets, some of which are physical and some of which are spiritual.

The 15/6 is here in service for their spiritual advancement. The numbers are beginning to be fewer: 96/69, 87/78. This is not a usual number to find in the world at this time and much responsibility is implied.

The 16/7 gives openings for new levels of consciousness. The only three numbers are 97/79 and master number 88. These numbers are a privilege to have, but difficult to live up to. Much is expected from these numbers in the way of spirituality in this earth living, especially the master number 88 with its inherent double power number.

The 17/8 shows spiritual power ending—98/89, with only two numbers available at this time. It is the highest lesson on using spiritual power within the physical arena available to us within this set of numbers, and has the nine of completion within it.

The only 18/9 on the spiritual side is master number 99 which, I believe, is an ending number for lessons and growth in this incarnating environment, and is a powerful power point for growth in the next continuum. It is two nines and reduces to a nine. It is a completion within the cycle of nines and within the cycle of 99.

Donna Linn

The spiritual side of the triangle uses those numbers which reduce to the teen numbers before the single digit numbers.

My interpretation of these numbers is as follows:

19/91—end of cycle of self-understanding and leadership
28/82—aiding unity through balance and ambition/authority
37/73—aiding unity through cooperation and spiritual awareness
46-64—aiding unity through physical power and responsibility/service
55—master number for leadership; aiding unity through much change

29/92—end of cycle of duality within a spiritual context
38/83—aiding balance through cooperation and spiritual authority
47/74—aiding balance through physical creation and spiritual awareness
56/65—aiding balance through adaptability and service

39/93—end of cycle of lessons in association and cooperation
48/84—aiding cooperation through using physical and spiritual power
57/75—aiding association through adaptability and spiritual awareness
66—master number, aiding association/cooperation through service

49/94—end of cycle of building solid foundations
58/85—learning to build solid foundations through change and spiritual power
67/76—learning to build solid foundations through service and spiritual awareness

59/95—end of cycle of change
68-86—learning to deal with change through responsibility and spiritual power
77—master number, aiding change through spiritual awareness

69/96—end of cycle of responsibility
78/87—learning spiritual awareness within a power context

79/97—end of cycle of spiritual opening/awareness
88—master number—aiding spiritual awareness for others through a double dose of authority—giving help to those who are newly learning

Breaking the Code

89/98—end of cycle of right use of power (spiritual or physical)

99—master number—end of cycle of this level of learnings—a negative coordination point.

I believe the first 18 numbers (center of the parallelogram) encompass all the spiritual lessons humanity has to learn. The numbers that reduce to these are important within their own right as nuances of the major numbers and different aspects of the main number 10, 11, 12, 13. The 14, 15, 16, 17, and 18 are important because less seen, have been given much responsibility, with 18 being a strong coordination point for future growth.

As we work on names and birth dates for individuals, we find that a chart sometimes contains numbers over 99. We use the same meanings, just more nuances for the number, more lesson working within the main number.

The only exceptions to these are the numbers that follow and what I believe them to mean:

100—bring much change in the way of thinking of self—as part of unity
110—bring balance through much self-discovery
120—bring groups together through self-discovery and balance
130—bring building blocks together as a foundation for self for self-discovery, and growth within groups
140—bring adaptability to change, more flexibility through self-discovery within a solid foundation
150---bring service and responsibility through self-discovery and change
160—bring spiritual unfolding through self-discovery and service
170—bring authority in spiritual places through self-discovery and spiritual path work
180—bring the hierarchal plan to fruition through self-discovery and spiritual power
190—end of cycle of self-discovery and new beginning

Chapter 5

NUMBERS AS CIVILIZATIONS

Each letter in your name has a specific reason for being there. The first name (and middle if you use it—Mary Ann, Jenny Sue) shows the lessons to be learned in this lifetime. The last name indicates the civilization and/or relevant lifetimes appropriate to lessons being learned, i.e., funneling good or bad karma and situations through which to work. As the name changes, then different learning and lifetimes apply. When one takes a different name, then different learning and lifetimes apply. In the new name, a totally new set of lessons and lifetimes are brought in to help in this lifetime's lessons. If it is used publicly (legal name change, marriage, etc.), the new lessons apply.

Each civilization that we have had on earth has had one distinctive, highlighted, characteristic to be learned through living at that time. Every lesson could be learned more easily at that time, although not at all impossible to learn at any other time. Each number also has another lesson that has been learned through several of these civilizations. It was usually learned over more than one lifetime and can be activated as an adjunct to the other lessons of the number. Many lessons perhaps are still being perfected. There are two major lessons and two major civilizations that belong to each number. These are my interpretations and are subject to change as more information becomes available. They are not like the ones in other books.

One: The number of "I am", of finding your place in the universe. As the number "One" is the "I am" number, it also plays an important role in teaching leadership in all its functions. It usually is learned temporally—in charge of an extended family, a group of people, a clan, a city, nation, or as part of the religious form of that particular period. Those coming into incarnation with leadership abilities have developed their abilities within the context of other lifetimes. It belongs to Zen and to the Mystery Schools.

Two: The two is the number of duality, of searching for balance. The lesson is learning to walk the middle way between things of earth and things of spirit. Many of these people are now even-tempered. Most of the problems they encounter are dealt with by solving the problem, not the dramatics of depression or "highs". It belongs to the Amerindian civilization and Space.

Three: The three is the number of cooperation and association. It involves working with many types of people in a cooperative grouping for the betterment of the group—not necessarily for the individual. The threes believe strongly in a faith held within the group. It belongs to the Chinese civilization, aborigines, and primitive tribes, also different forms of witchcraft.

Four: The number four is the number of building foundations, creating physically and physical power. It brings down the ability to build—both structures and communities by laying down firm foundations using the lessons of one, two, and three. It is a creative number, because many things need to be rebuilt on stronger foundations. It is physical, in that it encompasses all material objects built by man, from the smallest transistor to the largest building. It belongs to the Jewish civilization, especially at the time of the beginning of the Quaballa, and the Roman civilization.

Five: The five is the number of flexibility, change, and freedom. Nothing stays the same, all things change. The number five has the privilege to flow with this movement and become adaptable in all kinds of situation. It is also the lesson of taking our own responsibility and giving everyone around you his/her own responsibility. Before moving from this number, each person will be living his/her own life, taking his/her own responsibility for actions while not imposing restrictions on any other person. It is a number that is exactly in the middle of the lessons and while many have learned parts of the lesson, all must be mastered before entering the new realm. Much of this is the reason for the new lifestyles, the new "liberalisms" and the new ways of doing things we have now. As master of the number five, one must be adaptable to new situations, not griping or complaining, but pitching in, to make each change the best possible change for the group of individuals involved—not only Self. It belongs to the Buddhist and Greek civilization, as well as our own.

Six: Responsibility and service is the lesson of six—service to your fellowmen, on every level, and runs the gamut of service from family to universe with all places in between. This service can also be on any of the three levels—conscious, subconscious, and supra-conscious. Each level of consciousness, each level of grouping physically—family, neighborhood, city, state, nation, world, universe—has its own lessons of service to teach to those who are ready to learn and each person will be given the opportunity to learn each phase of service and responsibility at the proper time. Sixes believe in miracles. It belongs to the civilizations of Lemuria and Tibet.

Seven: Seven is the number of spiritual awareness, understanding, and unfolding. This is the unfolding of the spiritual life. It is the beginning of spiritualizing all of life—of becoming aware that all of life is part of one whole. It involves becoming consciously aware of one's self as a spiritual being, connected with all others. It is not a particularly strong formally religious person, although formalized religion may open up vistas through which they can first understand spirituality. There are as many parts to this lesson as there are spiritual paths. Each of them has its place and gives help to aspirants in that part of the lesson it teaches. Sevens are learning that we are all part of each other, and that we are all ONE. It belongs to the temples of Egypt and the South American Indians.

Eight: The number of spiritual power, of renewal and rebirth is the number eight. It is the internalization—the knowing and application—of the growth that has already taken place. It is learning how to manifest what one needs and how to use power for the spiritual good of the whole. The eight is the power one is able to access in the Universe. It requires working together of both physical and mental vibrations and ends with either a renewal or rebirth to the spiritual function of life, or a return to the lower numbers for a "refresher" course in the lessons not applied correctly. The eight is the Phoenix before the final lesson. It is the number of the Atlantean civilization and perhaps early Moslem times.

Nine: Nine is the number of spiritual completion and ascension. This is combining all previous numbers into a complete pattern of harmony. It is the vocation of the nine—Universal Love—to bring together both physical and spiritual reality into a community of love and caring. It completes the first cycle of numbers, but also encompasses all human needs and wants, with the universal, group consciousness. At the end of the nine cycle, all learning is reviewed to find any weak spots either of learning or application.

If all is well, one can become part of those who work with the people who have not completed all the lessons of their numbers. It is the number of Shamballa—the astral city said to be above the Gobi desert, and the Hierarchy.

There are also philosophies in the religious forms of worship that belong to each number. One equals truth. Ones are looking at religion with truth as the ultimate goal. Everything is black or white. The religious worship preferred by number two is shamanism. A shaman is a wise man (or woman) who is considered to have extraordinary powers and to see more clearly than the average person. He/She knows healing and can heal both physical and spiritual bodies through harmony.

The threes use association and movement as a spiritual force. With the lessons of physical building, fours need a guide book: they use the Kaballah, the Bible and other religious texts. With fives, change and freedom numbers tend toward accepting all forms of religion, and they investigate all religious forms.

Sixes accept responsibility for and service to all religious patterns. The sevens worship the sun god through intermediaries of priests and priestesses. The power source for this worship is the pyramid which magnifies the vibrations of love and worship. Eights use power of religion and power of the crystals. Nines know all is ONE and do not need any formalized religious ritual except their own.

Each number also carries with it a talisman and a color. The rainbow fits within the number system quite well. If one looks to the choice of colors one wears, usually it will resemble the lessons to explore at that time. Each number also has a planet and zodiac sign which are found in the following chart. As before, these are my interpretations and do not necessarily agree with any other book.

The numbers within the first name (and middle if used) show the lessons to learn. If more than one of the name number, then it has much more emphasis than the others. Those numbers of the last name also show the civilizations from which we are deriving the group situations of our lives.

LESSONS	CIVILIZATIONS	RELIGIOUS FORM	SHAPE	PLANET	ZODIAC	COLOR
1. "I Am" Leadership	Mystery Schools	Truth, Spirit	period	Mars	Sun, Aries	Red
2. Balance Duality	Native American Space	Harmony Shamanism Interpretation of Language	scales	Mercury	Gemini Pisces	Orange
3. Creativity Association Activity Cooperation	Chinese Witchcraft Primitive Tribes	Sufi, Faith	triangle	Jupiter	Libra	Yellow
4. Create physically Building blocks Physical creativity Physical power	Jewish, Roman	Kaballah, Bible Healing	square	Earth	Taurus, Leo	Green
5. Change, Freedom	India Greek	Buddhist Different Languages	cube	Uranus	Sagittarius Aquarius	Blue
6. Responsibility Service	Tibet Lemuria	Tantra, Miracles	circle	Saturn	Virgo	Indigo
7. Spiritual understanding/awareness, spiritual path work	Egyptian S. Am. Indian	Sun God Prophecy	pyramid	Neptune	Scorpio	Purple
8. Renewal, rebirth Spiritual power Internal growth Ambition and power	Atlantean, Moslem	Crystals Knowledge	phoenix, caduceus	Pluto	Capricorn	Red-gold
9. Ascension, Vocation, Spiritual Completion Evolution	Shamballa Hierarchy	Wisdom Unconditional Love	star	Venus	Cancer	White

Chapter 6
MASTER NUMBERS

Certain of the numbers we use can be given the designation of master numbers. These numbers seem to have more impact on the lives of which they are a part. They are key points or lessons with more expected of the individual as a test or challenge. The master numbers give greater impetus to those lessons and changes of energy that facilitate learning the lessons we need to learn in order to return to the Creator. The numbers 11, 22, and 33 have been used for many years. Contemporary numerologists are now adding the idea that 44, 55, 66, 77, 88, and 99 are also master numbers. I have included not only all these numbers, but also the numbers 111, 222, 333, 444, 555, 666, 777, 888, and 999. Usually, if you find one double number, you will find at least one more—in the physical area or the inner area. These numbers are involved in changes in energy. They are transition numbers—changes will take place within the life as the challenge is either meet or not. Everyone gets the same lessons, but not necessarily in the same order.

All double numbers show pathways for these energy changes. Beginning with the first master number, the 11/2 is the opening of the pathway to return to the Source. The double numbers through 99 are based on the number 11 which is the opening pathway for all energy exchange and growth. It is the first double number, a prime number, a "self" number, a double beginning number. It is the key upon which will someday be found the beginning of creation and learning. The number 11 is the mastery of the first awareness cycle with much self-exploration and purposefulness, combined with the two of duality and balance to continue that knowledge to a higher awareness. It must learn self-mastery and leadership through the two of balance. It is knowing "consciously" of something beyond yourself and striving to find balance in at least one area of life, yet be able to see the "top and bottom" of this balance. It may not be verbalized by the individual, but is intuitively hunted, usually with little rest until it is found.

The 22/4 number masters physical foundations through the twos of duality and balance. This number is very balance oriented and tries to keep a firm foundation in every part of life. The 22 has to be very much in control of any and all situations with which he/she is involved.

The number 33/6 requires new levels of service. It is a mastery of awareness (even if not conscious), of service to the One—of helping mankind grow toward re-union with spiritual awareness. This number is very involved with groups (large or small) and service to others—although it can be, it may not necessarily be in what we tend to think of as service organizations. When the 33 arrives in the number profile, one should have already mastered the 11 and 22 (balance and basic foundations) to successfully pass the test of associations (of many or few people), cooperation and communication in a service oriented (6) direction. These opportunities will show up, but may not be recognized until after they have been dealt with.

The 44/8 is mastery of spiritual and business power, and the ability to use it for the good of the whole. It shows the ability to bring spirituality into physical reality as firm foundations. It tends to be in on the beginning of new movements and new buildings. The 44 is the spiritual authority number and uses the building blocks of four as foundations for these energy shifts. This is the last of the "easy" or usual double numbers that we see in the exoteric numerology books.

This set of four numbers encompasses the major tasks for the even numbers.

- 11/2—duality and balance through self-discovery
- 22/4—physical creativity and foundations through balance
- 33/6—service and responsibility through associations
- 44/8—spiritual power through building firm foundations

These four numbers work together (22+33, 11+44) to form the square of human-ness upon which all other lessons are added. Knowing about this gives impetus to cooperating with spiritual plans and going forward faster, rather than repeating the same lessons over and over.

The higher master numbers teach the lessons of the odd numbers. They also reduce twice as opposed to the even numbers that reduce only once.

- 55/10/1—self-knowledge, "I am" through much change
- 66/12/3—groups, communication through service and responsibility
- 77/14/5—change, flexibility through spiritual awareness
- 88/16/7—spiritual awareness through power
- 99/18/9—end-of-cycle, hierarchy, unconditional love

The number 55/10/1 is mastery of more awareness of the "I am" and finds that awareness in all things. It reduces to 10 which is another one and the zero which starts a new cycle. Doubling the five of freedom and change brings about the mastery of the "I am" on a higher level. Now the person becomes conscious of him/her/self as a person with a spiritual part and goes about trying many ways of fulfilling that empty space. This number begins to see the strings that attach us one to another and to all the other kingdoms—plant, animal, angel, deva, etc. It is the lesson of the "Oneness" of all things. There are many changes that give chances to master this lesson.

Sixty-six/12/3 is mastery of a higher form of the three of association. It is also the awareness of group action on a spiritual plane—that one cannot "go it alone". It works through the self-knowledge and balance of the number twelve toward mastery of the three of association and communication. It is a double service number working through leadership and balance toward associations and can find itself part of many different groups and scattered in many directions. This also seems to be a time of mastery for those who have misused groups in other times. The double service seems to be "penance" for not using the knowledge previously received in the proper manner.

The number 77/14/5 in the number-profile brings into your life a powerful set of circumstances which is to bring about a rebirth to spiritual things. It is a double hit of spiritual awareness transmuting to the five of change and freedom. The 77 draws upon the self-knowledge and firm foundations (14) to cope with many changes in those areas of life that find this number. It implies mastery of changes. The question seems to be: "Can you have spiritual awareness within a constantly changing environment?"

The 88/16/7 is using the mastery of spiritual knowledge and power previously learned to help others forge ahead with their own learning and spiritual awareness. It reduces to the one of self and the seven of spiritual opening. The self-knowledge and service (16/7) combine to open spiritual doors, with mastery and/or understanding of their teachings. It gives the outward appearance of a double dose of spiritual power, an intermediary number "I am" and service, finishing with the seven of spiritual awareness. In other words, if spiritual power plus spiritual opening doesn't put you on the path, probably nothing will! Those with an 88 are usually "priests", or doing the things that a priest does—counseling, rituals, etc., always in a service capacity.

With the number 99/18/9, the end of cycle, all comes to a focus as you begin to teach spirituality to those around you (even if you are not aware of it). You use the self-knowledge and spiritual power (18/9) of this number to end the first set of lessons and prepare for the new and more powerful ones. It is a final mastery of spiritual path work—a triple nine so to speak—the teacher, the judge—the final chance on the first level to learn the spiritual humility and growth that transmutes human-ness to an ethereal quality laced with the trust that all will go according to the Universal Plan and the actions are in the best interests of the Plan.

This number becomes a potential "jumper" to the realm of higher power numbers and higher mastery—all of which include more awareness of the totality of connected-ness and the growth toward becoming part of the ONE.

The numbers from 11 to 99 make up the first set of master numbers. When finished with these lessons you are presumed to have mastered all the lessons of the first level! Here again, I want to emphasize that all of this may be on a subconscious, conscious, or supra-conscious level. It is another way to wake up those who are sleeping through this incarnation.

There are other numbers which I also consider to be master numbers. They are in the higher level numbers and are seen only occasionally in this plane of existence. They are sometimes found in the complement number or in the film negative number of a chart. They are being used, but most times the person is not aware of it or how it is working. Each of these numbers does not use the 11 but 111 to go to the next higher group of master numbers. From 111, the higher numbers continue to bring greater conscious appreciation of the Universal Plan. Each of the higher numbers works with the 3-6-9 principles—association/cooperation, service/responsibility, unconditional love! These are the numbers of the sacred triangle of life through which we must all eventually return to the ONE

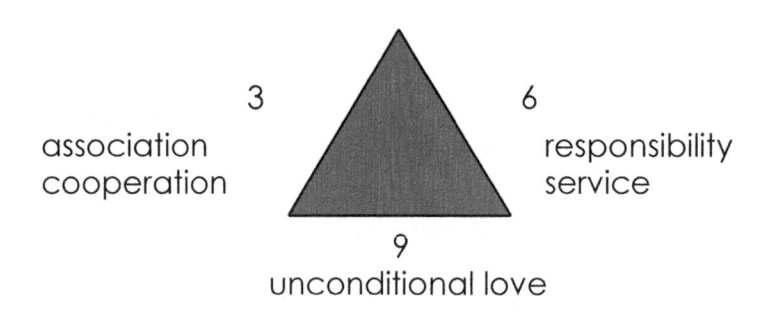

```
        3                          6
association                   responsibility
cooperation                   service
              9
      unconditional love
```

From 99, the higher numbers continue to bring greater conscious appreciation of the Universal Plan. The 111/3 understands and uses the "I am" modality to communicate that learning to groups of others. There is much learning about self involved here, but through groups of people. Perhaps this person would be in charge of the affairs of whatever group(s) he/she belongs. It is a higher mastery of the three of associations and cooperation.

The 222/6 has much balancing to do, but ends up on a service oriented mode. It has lessons in duality in many forms needing clear vision and balance. It is the next level of six—of service to the "One"

Because the 333 reduces to 9, it is another end of cycle number. People in many organizations and groups would work with this number. It is trying to find its way through many paths and groups to a spiritual completeness about life. This number never works alone. It is always associated with others.

The three fours (444/12/3) find this person detail-minded, grounded on foundations, but working through self-knowledge and balance as very important in group work. It would seem to be a strong physical building program through the cooperation of many people. This three brings much of the foundational work to associations and good communication among the group.

The three fives of 555/15/6 use the one of self-knowledge and the five of change working together to master the lesson of six—of service and responsibility. There is little but change in this life, and coping with the challenge of change in the way of service. This number must work on adaptability within a strong responsibility framework.

There is a very responsible quality about a person with the number 666/18/9. This number is always in a service and responsibility capacity. By working with self-knowledge and spiritual power (18/9), there is mastery of the number nine at a higher level. Much is written about the 666 of the Beast, or another name for man or humankind. It seems to me to be a potentially good number, using service to complete spiritual power and understanding of self with a final end-of-cycle number.

The number 777/21/3 shows spiritual awareness and understanding to be a very high priority, as are balance and self-understanding. This shows by the associations formed by this number, and the mastery of the three of associations and communications. Many spiritual paths become open through groups of people banding together.

The three eights (888/24/6) represent spiritual power used through balance and firm foundations to the highest mastery of the six of service. It seems to signify much spiritual authority becoming of service to the masses.

The 999/27/9 has only nines. The 27 of balance and spiritual path also reduces to another 9. It is the final master number and the end-of-cycle for this set of numbers. It is the total evolution, what we are aspiring to--the completion of our journey back to the One.

The master numbers give greater impetus to those lessons and changes of energy that facilitate learning the lessons we need in order to learn how to return to the Creator. There seems to be two paths for these master numbers. Many of us are working on both paths at the same time. They are completely different in energy. The numbers 11-99 are usually found in the physical numbers and beginning spiritual numbers. Each one carries the master lesson of exoteric numbers 1-9—how well we have mastered that part of our curriculum to date.

Breaking the Code 35

The master numbers divide into two sets. The first set is 11, 33, 55, 77, 99, 222, 444, 666, 888. Notice the double numbers are odd, while 222-888 are even numbers. The number 99 is the bridging number between physical and spiritual reality. It brings experiences that require you to hunt for a spiritual identity and become consciously aware of the spiritual body which controls the physical person, while ending that first cycle of numbers. You bring into yourself those experiences needed to show the way to spiritual awareness by the numbers of your name, nickname, and birth date. All is carefully chosen before birth, but you have freedom after birth to alter the plan of life previously made.

The second set is 22, 44, 66, 88, 111, 333, 555, 777, 999 with the bridging number of 111 for this group. Notice that these begin with the even numbers, then change to odd numbers. The original master numbers 11-99 equate to one master number for each numeral. This is not true for the higher master numbers. There are three 3-6-9 sets, one for each master number set. 111/3, 222/6, 333/9 is one set; 444/12/3, 555/15/6, 666/18/9 is the second set; and 777/21/3, 888/24/6, 999/27/9 comprise the last set. Notice also that 111-333 reduce only once, 444-666 reduce to teen number before single digits, and 777-999 reduce to 20s before the single digit.

Keep in mind that the 99 and 111 are bridging numbers. The sets are shown in the following chart. The intertwining pathway is as follows:

```
           4     8    12/3  16/7 \      3     9   / 15/6 \21/3  27/9
           22    44    66    88   \    111   333/  555  \777   999
          /\  / \   / \   / \    \    / \  / /\/  \ V  \  /
    11    33    55    77    99 \  /     222  /  444   666\  888
     2     6   10/1  14/5  18/9\          6  /  12/3  18/9 \ 24/6
```

Looking at these numbers, I feel that they are similar to the kundalini pathway in our body, with each number bringing more energy and knowledge to us.

Could this perhaps work with the chakra system as well? I submit this possibility, with the following numbers within the strings corresponding to the numbered chakra. Perhaps this is the placement of the first set of master numbers, 11-99. The placement of the chakra numbers would perhaps be as follows:

36 *Donna Linn*

1—base chakra—55/10/1
2—sacral chakra--11/2
3—solar plexus chakra—66/12/3
4—heart chakra—22/4
5—throat chakra—77/14/5
6—brow chakra—33/6
7—crown chakra—88/16/7
8—star chakra—44/8
9—the One—99/18/9

The upper master numbers from 111-999 are:

111/3	222/6	333/9
444/12/3	555/15/6	666/18/9
777/21/3	888/24/6	999/27/9

Now we have only three reduced numbers to use—3/6/9. There are very few of these numbers available within our physical world now, but many are in the unseen part of our numbers. The 3-6-9 series of master numbers indicates the place toward which we are all striving. It involves the three of association and cooperation with the six of service and responsibility and the nine of unconditional love. As we reach the 111-999 numbers, we are enveloping ourselves in the group, service, unconditional love characteristics that remind us of our true home, as part of the "One".

This second set of master numbers could then be divided into three parts. The first set, 111, 222, 333, would be the basic, physical work, the second set, 444, 555, 666, would be the intermediate work, with self-knowledge a a main component (within the reduced number—the one in ten's place, and the advanced set, 777, 888, 999, which uses balance (the two in tens place) as a main component.

These could also be seen as the 3-6-9 triangle-cooperation, service, love that will bring us back to the One—threes (111 physical, 444 physical/spiritual 777 spiritual), sixes (222 physical, 555 physical/spiritual, 888 spiritual), and the nines (333 physical, 666 physical/spiritual, 999 spiritual)

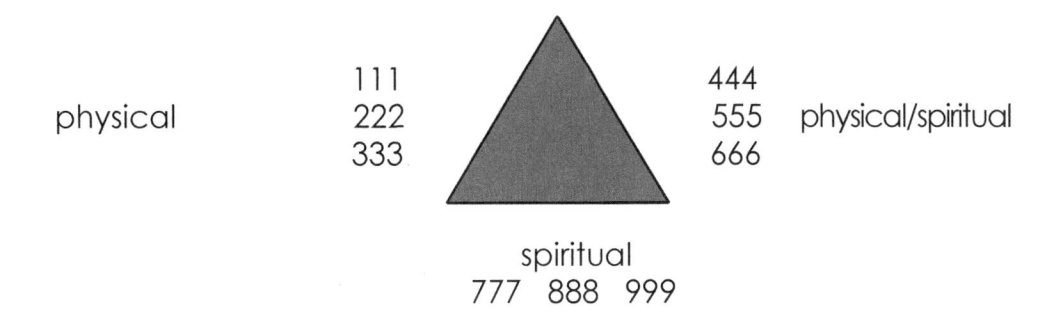

physical   111   444   physical/spiritual
              222   555
              333   666

spiritual
777   888   999

We can also divide them up according to number and therefore lesson.

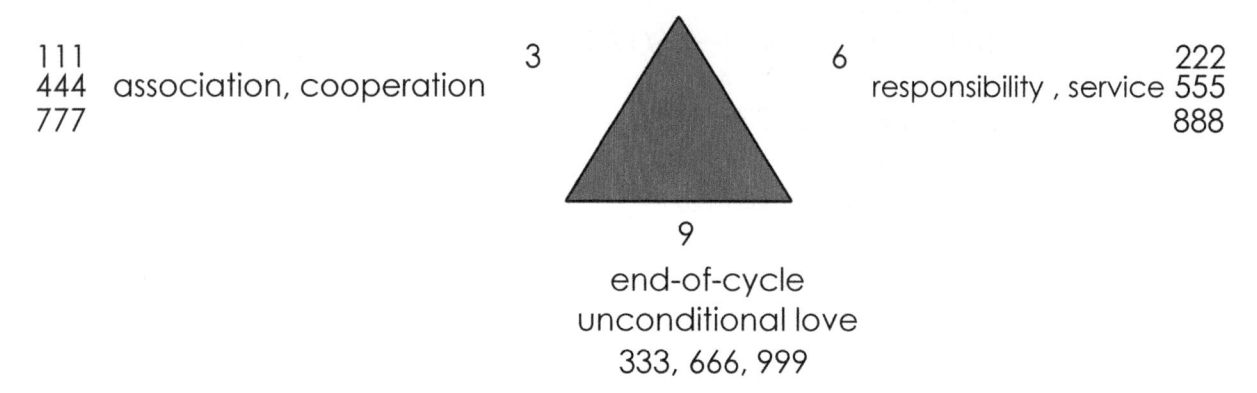

111
444 association, cooperation
777

3

6 responsibility , service

222
555
888

9
end-of-cycle
unconditional love
333, 666, 999

The master numbers can also be made into a square

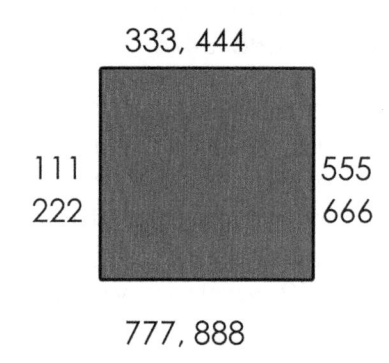

333, 444

111
222

555
666

777, 888

The 999 of unconditional love is the inside of the square.

The earlier master numbers can also be the same square. The only difference is that the 99 of endings is on the inside.

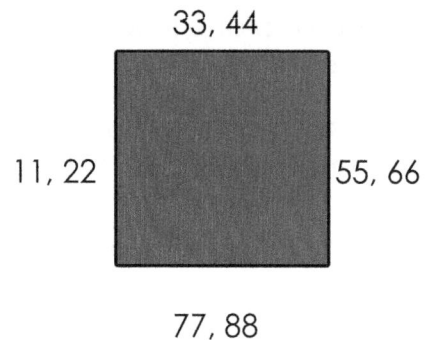

33, 44

11, 22

55, 66

77, 88

    If we look closely at these master numbers, we can also see how the master numbers work together to complete themselves. For instance, the first master numbers (11-99) can be shown as 11-88, 22-77, 33-66, 44-55—all end up as 99.

    The same way the master numbers 111-999 also do the same: 111-888, 222-777, 333-666, 444-555—all end up as the completion at 999.

Chapter 7
INITIATION NUMBERS

The complements of the master numbers I have termed initiation numbers. Each number found on the chart has one of these complement numbers showing the inner lesson being learned, but the only one that is an initiation number is the complement of a master number. To find the complementary number, just subtract that number from 10, 100, 1000. The complements of the master numbers are 11-89, 22-78, 33-67, 44-56, 55-34, 77-23, 88-12, 99-1, 111-889, 222-778, 333-667, 444-556, 555-445, 666-334, 777-223, 888-112, and 999-1. Sometimes the master number is on the inner plane and the initiation number is on the outer plane, or the master number is on the outer plane and the initiation number is on the inner plane.

The initiation, or other energy change number, is for specific changes within an individual. They can be utilized on a subconscious, conscious, or supraconscious level.

If the master number is seen, it shows on what lesson you are outwardly working, while the inner self is being challenged by the complementary lesson. If the master number is hiding, then the complementary number (an initiation number) is producing a challenge for the outer self.

The complement of 11, number 89/17/8, is on a "power trip" that must be transmuted into a pathway for growth. This is usually found through leadership with a spiritual focus. These two numbers, master number 11 and its complement 89, work together to make one part of the perfected whole.

The master number 22 has an initiation number of 78/15/6. It will be service oriented through spiritual awareness and spiritual power. There will also be a component of self and changes when dealing with this number. The number 67/13/4, the complement of master number 33 will have lessons of responsibility and spiritual openings using self-knowledge and cooperation toward the building number of four.

The complement of 44, number 56/11/2, is a composite number referring to both the eleven of self-knowledge and the two of duality and balance, while encompassing the five of freedom and change with the six of service. It is one of only two initiation numbers that shows another master number hiding within it-- because the 56 reduces to eleven before reducing again to the two.

This set of four numbers encompasses the major tasks for the even numbers. There is a master number and an initiation number for each of the single digit even numbers. In this group, the initiation number reduces.

- 11, 89/17/8—duality and balance; power and end of cycle
- 22, 78/15/6—physical creativity and building; spiritual opening and power
- 33, 67/13/4—associations, cooperation; service, responsibility and spiritual awareness
- 44, 56/11/2—building blocks, spiritual authority and power, change and responsibility

Numerology until now has not used the complements of numbers, nor called any of them initiation numbers. There may be a better name, but for now, I will call these particular numbers initiation numbers. They complement the master number with a powerful chance for change and growing, not only with the master, but also with the film negative of that number. It is a great "push" for learning the lessons of those numbers.

We have seldom used any master numbers except 11, 22, 33, and maybe 44. Now we seem to have been given an awareness of using the higher double numbers as master numbers, ready or not, and along with that, the initiation numbers which are the complementary numbers of the master numbers. It is as if the Universal Plan has said that we have had enough time to learn the simple lessons and must get on with our learning—preferably awake, but even if still sleeping.

The importance of using the complement number to see what is happening inside the ball or the film negative has become very important in learning the lessons in this incarnation now, at this time, not later.

The higher master numbers and their complements teach the lessons of the odd numbers.

55/10/1—45/9—much change of foundations; end of cycle number
66/12/3—34/7—cooperation, building blocks; spiritual opening
77/14/5—23/5—balance, cooperation; flexibility
88/16/7—12/3—self-knowledge with duality; cooperation
99/18/9—1—end of cycle, "I am"

Notice that the complement only reduces to a single digit, except for one that does not reduce at all, while the master number reduces twice.

The complementary number of 55 is initiation number 45—at the same time trying to finish one level of lessons (the nine) using a combination of foundations and change and also working with the 55's master of the one on the opposite plane. Initiation number 34, complement of the master number 66, is being tested on spiritual awareness and spiritual understanding through groups and cooperation and foundations of physical power even while major service and responsibility is attempted.

The 23, which is the complement of 77, is engaged in the lesson of how to use balance and association to create change, while the other plane is working on spiritual awareness. The initiation number of 12 uses the one of self with the two of duality to form groups with which the master number 88 may work on power on the opposite plane. It is just another piece of the perfected form of the numbers. The complement of master number 99 is the initiation number one, and the lesson become that of knowing and merging with the Universal "I am", the One while finishing up end of cycle work.

Within the first 99 numbers are all the lessons that humanity needs to learn before we can enter into a higher degree of learning, with the initiation numbers of 1, 12, 23, 34, 45, 56, 67, 78, and 89 being very important parts of the whole as complements to the master numbers. The key to all the lessons is HOW you react to the test, not when or if you pass or fail. If you pass, you continue on to the next set of lessons; if you fail, you return at another time to another test on the same material. You are responsible only for your own lessons, your own initiations, your own growth. No one else can know how you are progressing. Only you can accept or reject energy changes—except as they affect your before-of-age children. Then you accept or reject for your whole family. They can still decide whether to go along or not, but will usually follow at least until they are of an age to decide for themselves. Initiations can be easy or hard—in a short or long period of time—subconscious, conscious, or supra-conscious. They can involve meeting a person, going to a meeting, things at home. They are not usually known until after they have taken place. Again, they can happen subconsciously, consciously

Breaking the Code

or supra-consciously. The object of any spiritual path is to make you become aware of these changes, so that you can consciously accept these lessons and cooperate with the Universal Plan in order to return to the Source.

There are other master numbers explained in the previous chapter and as such, there are other initiation numbers. They include:

111/3—889/25/7	444/12/3—556/16/7	777/21/3—223/7
222/6—778/22/4	555/15/6—445/13/4	888/24/6—112/4
333/9—667/19/10/1	666/15/6—334/10/1	999/27/9—1

The master numbers above 99 are all 3-6-9 numbers. The initiation numbers are all 1-4-7 numbers. When working with the higher initiation numbers, we seem to be learning how to use the Oneness awareness, the building foundations, and spiritual path lessons to build a physical foundation for a spiritual pathway back to Oneness while the mastery numbers are giving us the self-understanding, cooperation, associations and service for the end-of cycle time.

The sevens include 889/25/7 which is the complement of master number 111/3. It is using spiritual power and end-of-cycle lessons through balance and change to bring about spiritual awareness. The 556/16/7, the complement of 444/12/3 is using much change and flexibility with responsibility through the "I am" path of self-awareness and service to bring this spiritual awareness into focus. The third initiation number is 223/7, the complement of master number 777/21/3. This number works through duality and groups toward the spiritual understanding and unfolding seen in all its parts.

The fours are all similar in nature, although they also use different patterns to get there. The end focus is building a very solid physical base upon which to build further bricks of learning. The 778/22/4 is the only other initiation number that has another master number embedded in it. It is the complement of 222/6 and does this by much spiritual learning and power through another master number (22). This number teaches using lessons of balance to end up with the 4 of physical foundations. It is building strong foundations through balancing of spiritual paths and spiritual authority, probably by bringing into physical existence those aspects which will help others to awaken spiritually.

The 445/13/4 is the complement of 555/15/6 and tries to push foundation building very hard by having the double four before the five of flexibility and change. It uses physical power and freedom to build the strong foundations and progresses to the four through self-development and cooperation. The 112/4 initiation number as complement of 888/24/6 uses the double self with balance to further building the solid foundation. It seems to be working toward using leadership to build physical success.

The ones begin with 667/19/10/1, complement of 333/6. It has within the interior of a person much responsibility, probably within groups, and spiritual growth with the outward showing master number 333/9 which is trying to master groups at end-of-cycle. Perhaps a leader (the 1 of 19, 1 of 10, and 1) of those groups trying to balance the self with Universal Love within a very much service oriented and spiritual character.

The 334/10/1 seems to be a new beginning on a much higher spiritual level using associations. The two threes of many people and four of foundations are growing toward leadership and the "I am" presence. The complementary master number is 666/18/9 and shows much service, much responsibility, and spiritual power leading to an end-of-cycle number 9.

The last number is "1". It is the complement of 999/27/9. It is a number seldom seen, but extremely important within the lessons that form the basis for returning to the One. It is the one and only lesson of the number one—learning about self and the "I am".

Here we also find three sets of 1-4-7. Notice that the one does not reduce and the 667 reduces twice. I have divided these numbers into three levels. The first set is physical and reduces only once; the second set is bridging the physical and spiritual and these numbers reduce twice. The third set seems spiritual.

The 667 reduces 3 times (the only one to do so) and the 778 and 889 reduce to the twenties before reducing again. There is only one master number to reduce into these number—the 22 embedded in the 778 initiation number.

Physical		Physical/Spiritual		Spiritual	
1	(999)	334/10/1	(666)	667/19/10/1	(333)
112/4	(888)	445/13/4	(555)	778/22/4	(222)
223/7	(777)	556/16/7	(444)	889/25/7	(111)

It seems to me that the first set is working strictly on the physical level—none of the three digit numbers reduce. The second set can be either physical or spiritual—as bridging numbers 10, 13, 16 (see parallelogram for discussion of the teen numbers) are intermediary numbers, or midway between three digit and one digit reduced.

The third set seems to be spiritual initiations. The 667 reduces three times—the only initiation number to do so. The 778 is the only one of the initiation numbers of the higher master numbers to reduce to a master number (22) within the reduction. The 889 also reduces to a 25, not a teen number, before reducing to seven.

Breaking the code

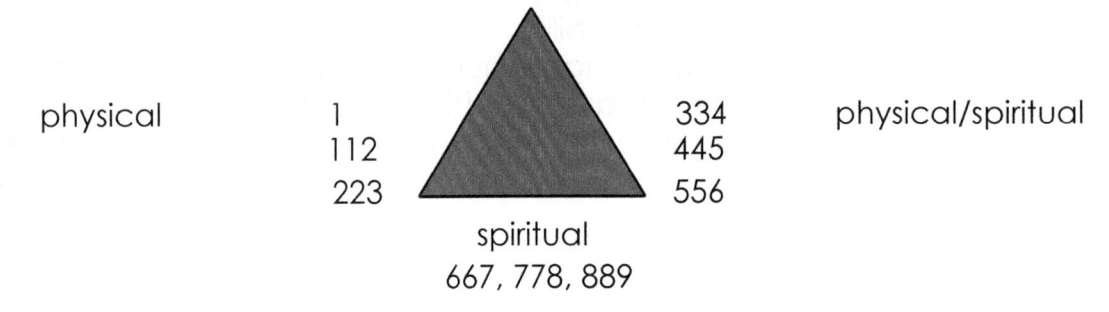

```
physical      1           334      physical/spiritual
            112           445
            223           556
               spiritual
             667, 778, 889
```

We can also label it according to the lesson given.

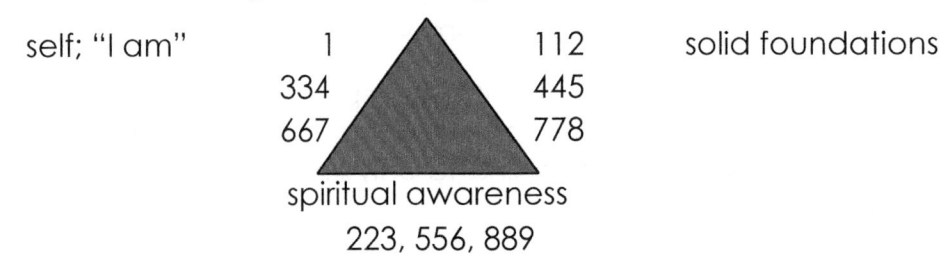

```
self; "I am"   1      112    solid foundations
              334     445
              667     778
            spiritual awareness
              223, 556, 889
```

These numbers can also be considered in a square format.

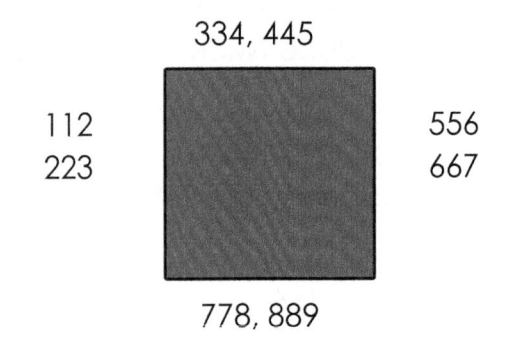

```
              334, 445
        112              556
        223              667
              778, 889
```

Another square using the same numbers in the 1-99 initiation numbers is as follows.

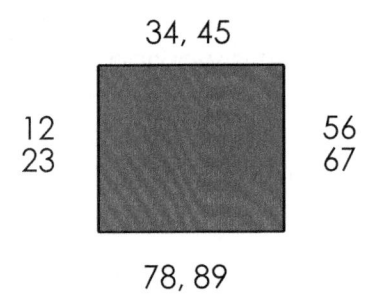

```
              34, 45
         12              56
         23              67
              78, 89
```

Another way is to add the numbers 12-89, 23-78, 34-67, 45-56. Each of this series adds to 101—a jump to the higher level lessons.

This can also be done with the 111-999 complement numbers 112-889, 223-778, 334, 667, 445-556. My guess is that they coordinate to an even higher level of lessons.

Chapter 8

HOW TO INTERPRET THE CHART

Your name as used by most people contains the lessons you are to learn at the present time. Your name holds your lesson plan and by changes in it, you change the lessons to be learned. If there is a name change (marriage, legal, adopted, etc.) other lessons will come into play.

The numbers of your name at birth and date of birth are key to the understanding of your intended plan for this lifetime and of other important lifetimes that are "carryovers" until now.

The birthdate is the life plan. To find this, one should add the month, the day, and the year, i.e. November 27, 2000 as 11+27+2=40/4. Many books delineate very well the four as a life number. My only suggestion would be to consider the 40 as a combination of firm foundations and a new beginning level of lessons. The same would be true with a birth date of April 1, 1966 which equals 4+1+(1+9+6+6=22) =27/9. Consider also the 22 of the year and the 27 before it reduces to 9.

The name has many important numbers. To start out, add all the vowels to get the soul number, all the consonants to get the outer personality number, add both together to get the destiny number, and add both the life number and the destiny number to get the power number. Subtract the vowels from the consonants to get the psychic number and the life number from the destiny number to get the center-self number.

The destiny number, in addition to the power number, gives an indication of the type of energy with which a person has come into this life. If the destiny number is not the same as the power number, or next to it (5-4, 3-4, etc.) it seems to be an "old energy" (5-3, 2-7) working out old energy patterns not previously completed. If the destiny number is next in line to the power number (3-2, 2-3, 8-9, 9-1), then one is in a "transition" energy pattern and has the opportunity, with a name change, to become part of a "new" energy pattern. Those with both destiny and power numbers that are the same start out with "new energy" patterns, but can choose not to accept this pattern and change it by changing the name used.

Life numbers one and eight also seem to be transition numbers, while any life number of nine seems to be not only end-of-cycle, but also bringing in "new" energy to this lifetime. I have found that even when the numbers themselves change by names or nicknames, the rotation does not seem to change, i.e., old energy 1-4, 9-6, or transition energy 3-4, 7-8, 9-1, or new energy 3-3, 4-4, 9-9. Sometimes a married name or complete change of name will change the numbers from old to transition, from transition to old, from transition to new, or from new to transition numbers. I have not seen them change from old to new or new to old. It seems that you must go through a transition number before "new" energy can come in to this life.

The numbers that are missing from any place within the name or major numbers seems to mean that those lessons need to be learned. They are also the key to family connections. The numbers in your first name are the civilizations from which you are drawing lessons into your life, while the numbers in the last name are group lessons.

How we get the numbers is very important. Let's review the exoteric numbers: 1-ajs, 2-bkt, 3-clu, 4-dmv, 5-enw, 6-fox, 7-gyp, 8-hqz, 9-ir. One rule I use for vowels: If two vowel letters make one sound, consider both as vowels. This includes the w and y. If the y takes the place of a vowel or is phonetically a vowel, consider it a vowel: Jerry—the e and y are vowels. Olivia, the O, I, and ia are all vowels. On the same page, put down the birth date and add the month, date and the addition of the year, i.e., September 22, 1941=September (9), 22 (never reduce an 11 or 22), and 1941=1+9+4+1=15/6. Exoterically this birthdate is 9+22+6= 37/10/ 1 and uses the life pathway of 1. Esoterically this birthdate is 9+22+15=46/10/1. The only difference is that it uses the 46 and 10 as a part of the life path 1 instead of just the one.

On the last page of this chapter, I have put together a chart to bring all the information together in a coherent package to look at and help find all relevant numbers. Put in the birthdate and add it together both as a single digit and complete number. Find the complement number and write it in the proper space.

On the line with the x, print the name to be looked at (the middle row). Then put the numbers 1-9 above for the vowels and below for the consonants. On the top line above the vowels, use the full numbers (a-1 and z-26) and at the bottom give each consonant the full number.

Under the name, put 1—the original birth certificate name, 2—any other names (possibly a married name, a nickname), 3—the name as used most often if different from the signature name, and/or 4—nickname—first and last.

Add all the numbers of the first line above the name and then add all the numbers of the second line above the name. These numbers will give the soul number exoterically (first row) and esoterically (upper row). Then add all the numbers below the name—first row exoteric, second (bottom) for esoteric.

Add the vowels and consonants together to get the destiny number. Add the destiny and life numbers for the power number. Next, subtract the vowels from the consonants for the psychic number and subtract the life number from the destiny number for the center-self number. Now find the missing numbers from the name.

At this time, a calculator comes in very handy! Add each name separately and just above or just below the numbers added. If your addition is correct, the second set of numbers will reduce to the original 1-9 set. Put a parenthesis around the usual first name or names, i.e., (Mary), (Mary Ann).

When all the numbers have been added, use columns for birth date, vowels, consonants, destiny, power, psychic self, center self and missing numbers. Fill in the columns with the correct same sequence numbers from the top numbers. Be sure that each set of numbers (exoteric and esoteric) reduce to the same base number. When reducing numbers, be sure to put in all steps, i.e., 46/10/1. This becomes a double check of the correctness of your addition (I need this a lot!). I use a blue or black pen, or a pencil.

Then go through all columns to look for important numbers—repetition, opposite numbers for the same name (13, 31) Find all numbers ending in zero, master and initiation numbers and mark them (I use different color highlighters).

The next step is to use a red pen to find the complement numbers (subtract from 10, 100, 1000) and put them in the same block, but smaller. Look for any numbers that end in zero, any master numbers, initiation numbers, any numbers that are opposites, and mark them in highlighter colors, also.

Now go back to the top and add each individual name numbers together and find their complement. Sometimes you find opposites and complements here that are important, too.

Find out what numbers are missing within the name and put it under the column called "missing". From the families that I have done, it seems that the missing numbers indicate the soul family with which you are working. Most times husband and wife will have at least one similar missing number. If not, the marriage will have many ups and downs, due to the different lessons being learned. These missing numbers also seem to belong to groups of people who incarnate at the

Breaking the Code 47

same time, as you can see by doing a family picture—grandparents, parents, children, grandchildren. Most times, the children will have the same missing number(s) of at least one of the parents and will prefer this parent.

If there are different numbers missing in the child's chart, he/she will have a difficult time with the parents. If no numbers are missing in the child's chart, I believe that he/she has come back as support for one or both of the parents. A child "belongs" to the parent of the missing numbers, or the power number energy. As the child grows up and out of the original family, he/she will change or shorten that name so that the individual lessons needed to learn in this lifetime show up.

The missing numbers in the first name (or first and middle if used) show what individual lessons are scheduled for this lifetime. If more than one of the same number, then it has more emphasis than the others. These show the civilizations from which we are deriving some of the situations of our lives. The missing numbers in the last name change only as the last name changes—at which time the soul family lessons also change. I have not made a chart for family numbers, because it depends on how many names you are using. There are bookkeeping forms on the internet that work quite nicely.

Looking through the numbers on the chart, one should look for similar numbers. Begin by looking at the 1-9 reduced numbers within the birth name and "current use" name. If any are the same, the lesson is stronger. Then look at the numbers with zeros. If there are no numbers that end in zero, there are no new beginnings. Perhaps if there are no beginnings, we do not stay too long, or we are just cleaning up old lessons. Look for master numbers (11, 22, 33, 44, etc.), for opposite numbers (34-43, etc.) that are the same lesson. Check for numbers that reduce twice (spiritual path) versus numbers that reduce immediately to one through nine (physical path). Circle the numbers within the parallelogram. Then look at the complement numbers to find hidden information on master numbers, initiation numbers, end in zero numbers, end-of cycle numbers).

These are the only numbers I use to delineate a reading:

1. LIFE and DESTINY numbers work together to see where you are headed
2. SOUL gives an indication of inner work
3. OUTER PERSONALITY shows "you" to the world
4. POWER indicates how your life and destiny numbers can play out
5. If the PSYCHIC SELF is a minus number, intuition and "knowing" come easily: if it is 0-9 "knowing" takes a little work, if 10-19 it can be acquired with some work; 20+ will be more difficult.
6. The CENTER SELF is that core of light in the center of your being. It seems to show those lessons already mastered.
7. MISSING numbers are not only karmic numbers, but direct whole families toward lessons needed

8. Use the PARALLELOGRAM to chart the column numbers. Look to see if there are more physical or spiritual numbers or about the same number. Remember the teen numbers can be on either the physical or spiritual side.
9. An "eleven" anywhere shows where growth will be possible first. It is a pathway previously developed to use to grow during this lifetime. It implies a purposeful-ness to this area. A "22" will show which pathway you are on already.
10. Any number over 99 is the next level of growth. As I understand it, there seems to be nine levels of growth (100s, 200s, etc.). Some show up physically, some on the film negative numbers.
11. If a number is REPEATED, learn the lesson or else!
12. Repeat numbers 1, 2, 3, 4 with the film negative numbers.

This chart brings into focus what lessons you have brought into this world to learn during your tenure here on earth. There seems to be nine points of energy—for change within a lifetime blueprint. These are every nine years with major energy focal points at 18 years, 45 years, and 72 years.

The eighteen year point can be seen as a division between childhood and adulthood. Your parents or guardian are responsible for your actions in the outer world until 18, although by age 16 you become pretty much responsible for yourself—under their authority. At 18, the child becomes an adult and is responsible for himself or herself—getting a job, going to college, getting married and taking the consequences of all his/her own actions. During the period of 18-45, we finish higher education, become a participating member of society, and have a family which by the 45th birthday is usually mostly grown. At 18 there is a three year overlap—it can happen between 15 and 21; at 45 it is a five year overlap—between 40 and 50, before the changes in energy are manifested outwardly. Forty-five also seems to be the time when karma should be finished for this lifetime and service started. This is spiritual service toward the Universal Plan—even though the person is not aware of it and this can be subconscious, conscious, or supra-conscious. Forty-five is the time that many people begin new careers and new lives for themselves. Generally, at 54 we are at the top of our field and beginning to look for ways to change our life, but not necessarily totally and at 63 we begin to look forward to retirement. At seventy-two, in most cultures, we tend to look over what we have done, and begin to be the wise ones of the time within our area of expertise, within our culture.

0/9/18   27/36/45-- 54/63/72   81/90/99

0=new beginning (birth)
90=end-of-cycle, new beginning
99=end-of-cycle/recap of lessons 1-9

Breaking the Code

```
              0    |   99
Childhood     9    |   90      Elder
   ↓         18    |   81        ↑
              _____

             27    |   72
Adulthood    36    |   63      Maturity
   →         45    |   54        ↑
```

These energy points can also be a triangle.

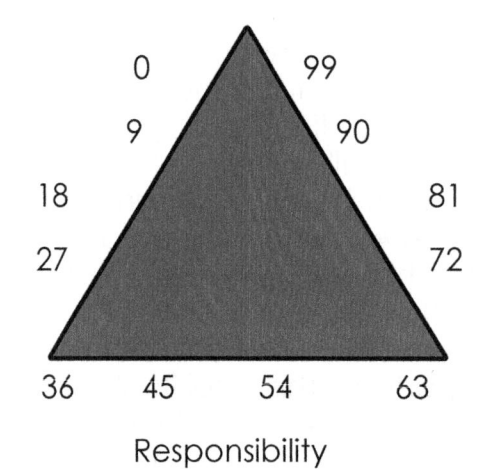

```
                        0    99
                         9  90
Growth              18        81      Elder knowledge
                  27            72
                 36   45   54   63
                    Responsibility
```

50 *Donna Linn*

Name _____ Date of Birth _____

_____
_____
x_____
_____
_____

NAME	DOB Life	VOWELS Soul	CONSONANTS Outer. Pers.	V+C Destiny	C-V	D+L Psychic	D-L Power	MISS Center

1 _____

2 _____

3 _____

4 _____

5 _____

Spiritual Numbers   Physical Numbers

91 82 73 64 55 46 37 28 19 10/1\10
    92 83 74 65 56 47 38 29 11/1\11 20
        93 84 75 66 57 48 39 12/3\12 21 30
            94 85 76 67 58 49 13/4\13 22 31 40
                95 86 77 68 59 14/5\14 23 32 41 50
                    96 87 78 69 15/6\15 24 33 42 51 60
                        97 88 79 16/7\16 25 34 43 52 61 70
                            98 89 17/8\17 26 35 44 53 62 71 80
                                99 18/9\18 27 36 45 54 63 72 81 90

Birth Date—Month _____   Place _____
           Day _____   Time _____
           Year _____

Breaking the Code 51

Name _____   DOB _____

What is seen and where—Outside	What is happening on the Inside
Master Numbers	Master Numbers
Complementary Numbers	Complementary Numbers
Opposite Numbers	Opposite Numbers
Beginnings	Beginnings
Endings	Endings

Spiritual vs. Physical Numbers

Psychic Self

Missing Numbers

Power Number	Power Number
Destiny Number	Destiny Number
Life Number	Life Number
Soul Number	Soul Number
Outer Personality Number	Inner Personality Number

Chapter 9
IMPORTANT YEARS

Each person has many significant things happen in their lives on all four levels of being—physical, mental, emotional, and spiritual. They can be things like changing houses, meeting new people, beginning or finishing a learning experience or even a dream. Marriage, children, divorce, and other important changes for each person can be detected—although many times not specifically which until you look back. Then you can say, "Oh, yes, that year was when... happened." Each part of your life can be profiled, but not all years will be as important as others. It can be subconscious, conscious, supra-conscious—while the only part we can relate to is the conscious part.

Sixteen sets of numbers are important within your profile. Four sets deal with the physical body, four sets with the mental body, four sets with the emotional body, and four sets with the spiritual body. To find each of these you will need the time and date of birth, and where that person was born. Next is a very simplified version of how to get each of the first eight sets of numbers. It is explained more fully later in the chapter.

PHYSICAL—regular date of birth

   1. Hour + minute of birth

   2. Day + year

MENTAL—regular date of birth

   1. Day

   2. Month + day

C. EMOTIONAL—regular date of birth
  1. Month
  2. Month + year

D. SPIRITUAL—regular date of birth
  1. Year
  2. Month + day +Year

The next eight sets of numbers use the time of birth transferred to Greenwich mean time, or Universal Time. This, for me, was the hardest part. I knew there was another set of numbers, but they were very hidden from me, especially the physical sets. It took lots of work to figure them out, but when I did, I knew they were very important.

FROM UNIVERSAL TIME

E. PHYSICAL—universal time
  1. Hour + minute of birth
  2. Day + year

F. MENTAL—universal time
  1. Day
  2. Month + day

G. EMOTIONAL—universal time
  1. Month
  2. Month + year

H. SPIRITUAL—universal time
  1. Year
  2. Month + day + year

These numbers and how to get them is addressed in the following part of this chapter.

A. PHYSICAL

For example, using the birth time of 12 hours 24 minutes p.m., we add them together and reduce them as many ways as possible. 12+24=36/9; 3+24=27/9; 12+6=18/9; 3+6=9. All reduce to nine (a check on my math). For a birth time of 9:50 a.m., we would add 9+50=59/14/5; 9+5=14/5. If the birth time was 5:16 p.m., we would use the 24 hour clock to make it 17 hours and 16 minutes, or 17+16=33/6; 8+16=24/6; 17+7=24/6; 8+7=15/6. Take each year and add three ways—down, across, any reduced number.

1. Hour + minute: 12:24=12+24=36/9; 3+24=27/9; 12+6=18/9; 3+6=9

Add each of these numbers, 36, 27, 18, and 9 to the year of birth (in this case 1941).

1941↓	1941→	1941r	1941↓	1941→	1941r
36	36	36	27	27	27
1977	1977	1977	1968	1968	1968
36	24	6	27	24	6
2013	2001	1983	1995	1992	1974
36	3	3	27	21	3
2049	2004	1986	2022	2013	1977

Continue until you have reached approximately 100 years (or 2041)

Do the same for 18 and 9.

1941↓	1941→	1941r	1941↓	1941→	1941r
18	18	18	9	9	9
1959	1959	1959	1950	1950	1950
18	24	6	9	15	6
1977	1983	1975	1959	1965	1956
18	21	3	9	21	3
1995	2004	1978	1968	1986	1959

And so on for approximately 100 years.

2. Next, we use the day plus the year—in our example it is 9/22/41. Add together and reduce to the lowest number.

Day + year   22+1941 (1+9+4+1=15/6)   22+15=37/10/1; 4+15=19/10/1; 22+6=28/10/1. In this case, I use the 37, 28, 19, 10 (once), and one (once).

1941↓	1941→	1941r	1941↓	1941	1941r
37	37	37	28	28	28
1978	1978	1978	1969	1969	1969
37	25	7	28	25	7
2015	2003	1985	1997	1994	1978
37	5	5	28	23	5
2052	2008	1990	2025	2017	1983

Continue for approximately 100 years.

Breaking the Code

1941	1941	1941	1941	1941	1941
19	19	19	10	10	10
1960	1960	1960	1951	1951	1951
19	16	7	10	16	7
1979	1976	1967	1961	1967	1958
19	23	5	10	23	5
1998	1999	1972	1971	1990	1963

Continue up to 100 years.

1941	1941	1941
1	1	1
Every year	1942	1942
	16	7
	1958	1949
	23	5
	1981	1954

And so on until approximately 100 years

    To find the other two important sets of years for physical dates, we take the date and year of birth and put it to one side—i.e., 9/22/41. Take the time (12:24 p.m., EST. and change the time using a 24 hour clock so we can get Greenwich time, or Universal Time. This is done by adding the number of hours away from Greenwich, England—EST, add 5 hours, CST, add 6 hours, MST, add 7 hours, PST, add 8 hours, and then add 10 seconds for every hour added for the differences in longitude. If on daylight time at birth, we must subtract one hour—EDT adds only 4 hours (5 hours minus 1 hour), CDT subtract 5 hours, MDT subtract 6 hours, PDT subtract 7 hours. So the birth at 12:24 p.m. EST would still be 12:24, while 2:30 p.m. would be 14:30 (using the 24 hour clock). Then add the hours away from Greenwich: EST—12:24+5 hours =17 hours; CST—2:30 (14:30+6 hours =20:30, or 20 hours, 30 minutes. Add 10 seconds correction for each hour of Greenwich time to the number previously found. For example: 12:24 p.m. EST is as follows:

12:24:00 p.m. EST=time of birth
 5:00:00   change in time from Greenwich, England
     :50   10 seconds per hour from Greenwich time—longitude change.
17:24:50   Universal Time

    If the birth time is 1:45 a.m. CST, we would have 1:45+6 hours 60 seconds, or 7 hours 46 minutes (60 seconds equals one extra minute). If it is 1:45 p.m. CST, we would start with 13:45 (24 hour clock), then add 6 hours and 60 seconds to get a Universal Time of 19 hours 46 minutes. If it is 10:30 p.m. EST, we have to change 10:30 p.m. E.S.T. to (24 hour clock) 22 hours 30 minutes plus 5 hours plus 50 seconds to equal 27 hours 30 minutes 50 seconds.

    Since an Earth day is only 24 hours long, we must subtract 24 hours from 27:30:50 and get the FOLLOWING day at 3:30:50 a.m. This becomes very important later in our calculations.

The Universal Time becomes the year, month, and day for the rest of the chart. For instance, in the original example, 12:24 p.m. EST, Universal Time becomes 17:24:50. The 17 hours would convert to 17 years, the 24 minutes would convert to months (procedure to follow), the 50 seconds convert to days (procedure to follow).

The 24 minutes equals months after dividing by five because we can have 60 minutes, but only 12 months. In other words, every 5 minutes equals one month. First, divide the 24 minutes by five to get four and four fifths months. The 4/5 of a month can be increased (4/5x6) to 24/30 days or 24 days. Therefore, 24 minutes is equal to 4 months 24 days.

Fifty seconds equals the number of days after dividing by two because you can have 60 seconds, but only 30 days (disregard 31 days in a month). Every two seconds equals one day. We find that 50 seconds divided by two equals 25 days.

In summary:
1. 17 hours=17 years
2. 24 minutes=4 months, 24 days
3. 50 seconds=25 days
4. Add 24 days+25 days (from 2 and 3 above)=49 days minus 30 days=1 month 19 days
5. Add 4 months+1 month (from 4 above)=5 months
6. Total=17 years, 5 months, 19 days

Using this birth date in its changed form, we can begin to find more important dates in our lives. Begin by using the Universal Time of birth for the next two sets. We will use the 17 years, 5, months, 19 days later.

3. Greenwich time: 17:24:50 CHANGES TO 17:25. When using hours and minutes, any seconds after 30 become another minute
17+25=42/6   8+25=33/6   17+7=24/6   8+7=15/6
Use only the 42, 33, 24, 15, and 6 (once).

1941	1941	1941	1941	1941	1941
42	42	42	33	33	33
1983	1983	1983	1974	1974	1974
42	21	3	33	21	3
2025	2004	1986	2007	1995	1977
42	6	6	33	24	6
	2010	1992	2040	2019	1983

Continue until approximately 100 years.

Breaking the Code 57

1941	1941	1941	1941	1941	1941
24	24	24	15	15	15
1965	1965	1965	1956	1956	1956
24	21	3	15	21	3
1989	1986	1968	1971	1977	1959
24	24	6	15	24	6
2013	2010	1974	1986	2001	1965

Continue for approximately 100 years.

1941	1941	1941
6	6	6
1947	1947	1947
6	21	3
1953	1968	1950
6	24	6
1959	1992	1956

And so on until approximately 100 years.

4. Greenwich time 17:24:50 DOB=17 years, 24 months, 50 days, changed to 17 years 5 months 19 days (as shown previously)

Day 17/8+year 19/10/1 using Greenwich time: 17+19=36/9, 8+19=27/9, 17+10=27/9, 8+10=18/9, 8+1=9 Chart the numbers 36, 27, 18, 9. Do not do both 27s or 9s.

1941	1941	1941	1941	1941	1941
36	36	36	27	27	27
1977	1977	1977	1968	1968	1968
36	24	6	27	24	6
2013	2001	1983	1995	1992	1974
36	3	3	27	21	3
2049	2004	1986	2022	2013	0977

And so on, until you reach approximately 100 years.

1941	1941	1941	1941	1941	1941
18	18	18	9	9	9
1959	1959	1959	1950	1950	1950
18	24	6	9	15	6
1977	1983	1965	1959	1965	1956
18	21	3	9	21	3
1995	2004	1968	1968	1986	1959

Continue until about 100 years.

All of the first four parts are connected with the physical part of the entity and all these dates are in some way important with the physical part of life. We will plot them later on a chart.

58 *Donna Linn*

In the same way, the next four parts play an important role with the mental part of the entity and are found as shown next.

MENTAL

To find the first part again use the birth date (9/22/41). Using only the day of birth, we begin with the year 1941 and add the days to it down, across and reduced if possible so you have three sets for each number (22 and 4)

1. Day 22/4

1941	1941	1941	1941	1941	1941
22	22	22	4	4	4
1963	1963	1963	1945	1945	1945
22	19	1	4	19	1
1985	1982	1964	1949	1964	1946
22	20	2	4	20	2
2007	2002	1966	1953	1984	1948

Continue until you reach 100 years.

2. This part uses the month plus the day added to the year of birth, then added down, across, and reduced if possible.

Month + Day   9+22=31/4; 9+4=13/4   Use the 31, 13, and 4

1941	1941	1941	1941	1941	1941
31	31	31	13	13	13
1972	1972	1972	1954	1954	1954
31	19	1	13	19	1
2003	1991	1973	1967	1973	1955
31	20	2	13	20	2
2034	2011	1975	1980	1993	1957

And on until approximately 100 years

1941	1941	1941
4	4	4
1945	1945	1945
4	19	1
1949	1964	1946
4	20	2
1953	1984	1948

Continue for 100 years.

Breaking the Code

3. Return to the Universal Time and find the day (19).   Day=19/10/1

1941	1941	1941	1941	1941	1941
19	19	19	10	10	10
1960	1960	1960	1951	1951	1951
19	16	7	10	16	7
1979	1976	1967	1961	1967	1957
19	23	5	10	23	5
1998	1999	1972	1971	1990	1962

Continue to 100 years.

1941	1941	1941
1	1	1
Every year	1942	1942
	16	7
	1958	1949
	23	5
	1982	1954

Continue adding years down, across and reduced for approximately 100 years.

4. From the Greenwich time, find the month and day. In our example we have 5 months + 19 days, 5+19=24/6; 5+10=15/6; 5+1=6 Use the 24, 15, and one 6

1941	1941	1941	1941	1941	1941
24	24	24	15	15	15
1965	1965	1965	1956	1956	1956
24	21	3	15	21	3
1989	1986	1968	1971	1977	1959
24	24	6	15	24	6
2013	2010	1974	1986	2001	1965

Continue on.

1941	1941	1941
6	6	6
1947	1947	1947
6	21	3
1953	1968	1950
6	24	6
1959	1992	1956

And so on for approximately 100 years.

All of these mental numbers will be charted at the end of the chapter.

EMOTIONAL

The emotional block dates begin by using the month of the birth date and again adds three ways—down, across, and reduced.

1. Date of birth—Month 9 Because it does not reduce, there is only one set of three numbers for this number.

1941	1941	1941
9	9	9
1950	1950	1950
9	15	6
1959	1965	1956
9	21	3
1968	1986	1959

Continue for approximately 100 years

2. Date of birth—Month + Year   9+(1+9+4+1=15) 15=24/6   9+6=15/6

Use the 24, 15, and 6

1941	1941	1941	1941	1941	1941
24	24	24	15	15	15
1965	1965	1965	1956	1956	1956
24	21	3	15	21	3
1989	1986	1968	1971	1977	1959
24	24	6	15	24	6
2013	2010	1974	1986	2001	1965

And so on for about 100 years.

1941	1941	1941
6	6	6
1947	1947	1947
6	21	3
1953	1968	1950
6	24	6
1959	1992	1956

Again, continue until 100 years.

3. From Universal Time use the month—5

Because five does not reduce, there is only one set of numbers

1941	1941	1941
5	5	5
1946	1946	1946
5	20	2
1951	1966	1948
5	22	4
1956	1988	1952

Continue for approximately 100 years.

Breakig the Code 61

4. Also, using Universal Time, use the month + year

5+17= 22/4; 5+8=13/4.   We use the 22, 13, and 4.

1941	1941	1941	1941	1941	1941
22	22	22	13	13	13
1963	1963	1963	1954	1954	1954
22	19	1	13	19	1
1985	1982	1964	1967	1973	1955
22	20	2	13	20	2
2007	2002	1966	1980	1993	1957

And so on for about 100 years.

1941	1941	1941
4	4	4
1945	1945	1945
4	19	1
1949	1964	1946
4	20	2
1953	1984	1948

Continue for 100 years.

This concludes the important emotional years. They are put on the chart at the end of this chapter.

The spiritual years are found in the same way—one and two use the date of birth and three and four use the Universal Time date of birth.

SPIRITUAL YEARS

1. Date of birth—Year   1941=15/6. Use both the 15 and the reduced 6

1941	1941	1941	1941	1941	1941
15	15	15	6	6	6
1956	1956	1956	1947	1947	1947
15	21	3	6	21	3
1971	1977	1959	1953	1968	1950
15	24	6	6	24	6
1986	2001	1965	1959	1992	1956

Continue for 100 years.

62 Donna Linn

2.Date of birth—month + day + year 9+22+15=46/10/1; 9+4+15=28/10/1;
9+22+6=37/10/1; 9+4+6=19/10/1   Use the 46, 37, 28, 19, 10, and 1

1941	1941	1941	1941	1941	1941
46	46	46	37	37	37
1987	1987	1987	1978	1978	1978
46	25	7	37	25	7
2033	2012	1994	2015	2003	1985
46	5	5	37	5	5
	2017	1999		2008	1990

And so on for 100 years.

1941	1941	1941	1941	1941	1941
28	28	28	19	19	19
1969	1969	1969	1960	1960	1960
28	25	7	19	16	7
1997	1994	1976	1979	1976	1967
28	23	5	19	23	5
2025	2017	1981	1998	1999	1972

Continue for 100 years.

1941	1941	1941	1941	1941	1941
10	10	10	1	1	1
1951	1951	1951	every year	1942	1942
10	16	7		16	7
1961	1967	1958		1958	1949
10	23	5		23	5
1972	1990	1963		1981	1954

Keep going for 100 years

3.Using Universal Time   year=17/8

1941	1941	1941	1941	1941	1941
17	17	17	8	8	8
1958	1958	1958	1949	1949	1949
17	23	5	8	23	5
1975	1981	1963	1957	1972	1954
17	19	1	8	19	1
1992	2000	1964	1965	1991	1955

Continue on approximately 100 years.

Breaking the Code 63

4. Using Universal Time month plus day plus year=5+19+17=41/5; 5+10+17=32/5; 5+1+17=23/5; 5+19+8=32/5; 5+10+8=23; 5+1+8=14 We use only the 41, one 32, 23, and one 5

1941	1941	1941	1941	1941	1941
41	41	41	32	32	32
1982	1982	1982	1973	1973	1973
41	20	2	32	20	2
2023	2002	1984	2005	1993	1975
41	4	4	32	22	4
	2006	1988	2037	2015	1979

Continue until approximately 100 years.

1941	1941	1941	1941	1941	1941
23	23	23	5	5	5
1964	1964	1964	1946	1946	1946
23	20	2	5	20	2
1987	1984	1966	1951	1966	1948
23	22	4	5	22	4
2010	2006	1970	1956	1988	1952

And so on until year 100.

IN SUMMARY:

The first two sets of each part (physical, mental, emotional, spiritual) use the time and date of birth (i.e., our example, 12:24 p.m. EST, 9/22/41). The third and fourth sets of each part involve the Universal Time date of birth as found previously (17h, 5m, 19d) This is more difficult because you need the time of birth and the standard/daylight time of birth. Then it has to be converted to the correct proportion of years, months, and days.

All the numbers add to the birth year (1941) in three ways—down, across, and reduce in all ways and then add to +/- 100 years (2041), a little above or below that number. I go to 100 years because not many people live and work more than this, but it can easily carry further.

Notice that each group of numbers follows the 9, 3/6, 1-2-4-8-7-5 pattern (discussed later). After plotting each year, you will notice many of the years are the same. Add the number of times it shows up in each column. .

Take the years you found from #1 Physical and plot them on these charts, then #2 physical, and #3 and #4 in the proper places. Do the same for mental #1, #2, #3, and #4. Emotional and Spiritual are same. It is important to keep them in the proper column in case you are interrupted while putting the numbers in. I usually write the year in the column, but can also use slashes. If the year comes up more than once (as in the beginning of the years (1941+15, 1941+6; make sure you notate this in some way. I usually use a star to denote the beginning years of each column. In doing charts, many of the years will be the same. These are the important years. Any time a year comes up within the physical, mental, emotional, or spiritual area more than five times, most people have found it to relate to a life event.

All the dates will be important in some respect, although it may take a backward look to discover what was important about that year---growth in awareness, a test, something internally that started us on another cycle of living—and even then some will not be known. The importance can be subconscious, conscious, or supra-conscious—and some years we think are important do not show up at all. Our idea of what is important is not necessarily truly important. Or—we have not yet found the combination of numbers that show us in what way the year was important. Bear in mind, it might be a year very important for soul growth rather than entity growth and change.

Worksheet   Date of birth data   Universal Time data

Physical
    1. Hour + minute of birth
    2. Day + year of birth
    3. Hour + minute Universal Time
    4. Day + year Universal time

Mental
    1. Day of birth
    2. Month + day of birth
    3. Day Universal Time
    4. Month + day Universal Time

Emotional
    1. Month of birth
    2. Month + year of birth
    3. Month Universal Time
    4. Month + year Universal time

Spiritual
    1. Year of birth
    2. Month + day + year of birth
    3. Year Universal Time
    4. Month + day + year Universal Time

Date	Physical 1	2	3	4	Mental 1	2	3	4
year								

	Emotion				Spiritual			
Date	1	2	3	4	1	2	3	4
Year								

Name

Year	SUMMARY Physical	happen?	Mental	happen?	Emotional	happen?	Spiritual	happen?

Chapter 10

IMPORTANT YEARS, PART 2

Here is another way to find important dates. They are found the same way as the previous sets were—using the new assumed date of conception. The same hour and minute continue to be the same as for the birth. These dates are found by using the date of birth and subtracting nine months and three days. Some examples include:

9/22/41 minus 9 mo. 3 da.=12/19/1940
11/3/65 minus 9 mo. 3 da.=1/30/1965
2/4/82 minus 9 mo. 3 da.=5/1/1981

The sets of data follow the previous rules found in Chapter 9. Here again, add the numbers down, across and reduce. Go up to approximately 100 years. Notice, also, how the numbers again repeat themselves, getting the important years of this incarnation.

PHYSICAL—Date of conception

1. hour + minute: 12:24=12+24=36/9; 3+24=27; 12+6=18; 3+6=9

1940	1940	1940	1940	1940	1940
36	36	36	27	27	27
1976	1976	1976	1967	1967	1967
36	23	5	27	23	5
2012	1999	1981	1994	1990	1972
36	28	1	27	19	1
	2027	0982	2021	2009	1973

1940	1940	1940	1940	1940	1940
18	18	18	9	9	9
1958	1958	1958	1949	1949	1949
18	23	5	9	23	5
1976	1981	1963	1958	1972	1954
18	19	1	9	19	1
1994	2000	1964	1967	1991	1955

2. day + year   19+1940 (14)=19+14=33/6

1940	1940	1940	1940	1940	1940
33	33	33	6	6	6
1973	1973	1973	1946	1946	1946
33	20	2	6	20	2
2006	1993	1975	1952	1966	1948
33	22	4	6	22	4
2039	2015	1979	1958	1988	1952

PHYSICAL—Universal Time

Use the same numbers as in the previous chapter, but add to the conception date. Always continue to approximately 100 years.

3. hour + minutes   17+25=42/6; 8+25=33/6; 17+7=24/6

1940	1940	1940	1940	1940	1940
42	42	42	33	33	33
1982	1982	1982	1973	1973	1973
42	20	2	33	20	2
2024	2002	1984	2006	1993	1975
42	4	4	33	22	4
	2006	1988	2039	2015	1979

1940	1940	1940	1940	1940	1940
24	24	24	6	6	6
1964	1964	1964	1946	1946	1946
24	20	2	6	20	2
1988	1984	1966	1952	1966	1948
24	22	4	6	22	4
2012	2006	1964	1958	1988	1952

2.day + year   19+17=36/9; 10+17-27/9;   1+17=18/9;   19 +8=27/9; 10+8=18/9; 1+8=9

1940	1940	1940	1940	1940	1940
36	36	36	27	27	27
1976	1976	1976	1967	1967	1967
	23	5	27	23	5
2012	1999	1981	1994	1990	1972
36	28	1	27	19	1
2048	2027	1982	2021	2009	1973

1940	1940	1940	1940	1940	1940
18	18	18	9	9	9
1958	1958	1958	1949	1949	1949
18	23	5	9	23	5
1976	1981	1963	1958	1972	1954
18	19	1	9	19	1
1994	2000	1964	1967	1991	1955

Remember to take all the additions in each column up to age 100 years +/- 5 years.

MENTAL—date of conception:

1.day   19/10/1

1940	1940	1940	1940	1940	1940
19	19	19	10	10	10
1959	1959	1959	1950	1950	1950
19	24	6	10	15	6
1978	1983	1965	1960	1965	1956
19	21	3	10	21	3
1997	2004	1968	1970	1986	1959

Breaking the Code 71

1940	1940	1940
1	1	1
1941	1941	1941
Every year	15	6
	1956	1947
	21	3
	1977	1950

2. date of conception—month + day

12+19=31/4; 3+19=22/4; 12+10=22/4; 12+1=22/4; 12+1=13/4; 3+10=13/4; 3+1=4
Use 31, 22 (once), 13 (once), 4.

1940	1940	1940	1940	1940	1940
31	31	31	22	22	22
1971	1971	1971	1962	1962	1962
31	18	9	22	18	9
2002	1989	1980	1984	1980	1971
31	27	9	22	18	9
2033	2016	1989	2006	1998	1980

1940	1940	1940	1940	1940	1940
13	13	13	4	4	4
1953	1953	1953	1944	1944	1944
13	18	9	4	18	9
1966	1971	1962	1948	1962	1953
13	18	9	4	18	9
1979	1989	1971	1952	1980	1962

MENTAL—Universal Time

3. Day   19/10/1

1940	1940	1940	1940	1940	1940
19	19	19	10	10	10
1959	1959	1959	1950	1950	1950
19	24	6	10	15	6
1978	1983	1965	1960	1965	1956
19	21	3	10	21	3
1997	2004	1968	1970	1986	1959

72 Donna Linn

1940	1940	1940
1	1	1
1941	1941	1941
Every year	15	6
	1956	1947
	21	3
	1980	1950

4.month + day   Universal Time   5+19=24/6; 5+10=15/6; 5+1=6

1940	1940	1940
24	24	24
1964	1964	1964
24	20	2
1988	1984	1966
24	22	4
2012	2006	1970

1940	1940	1940	1940	1940	1940
15	15	15	6	6	6
1955	1955	1955	1946	1946	1946
15	20	2	6	20	2
1970	1975	1957	1952	1966	1948
15	22	4	6	22	4
1985	1997	1961	1958	1988	1952

EMOTIONAL—date of conception

1.month   12/3

1940	1940	1940	1940	1940	1940
12	12	12	3	3	3
1952	1952	1952	1943	1943	1943
12	17	8	3	17	8
1964	1969	1960	1946	1960	1951
12	25	7	3	16	7
1976	1994	1967	1949	1976	1958

Breaking the Code 73

2. month+year   12+14=26/8; 3+14=17/8; 12+5=17/8; 3+5=8

1940	1940	1940	1940	1940	1940
26	26	26	17	17	17
1966	1966	1966	1957	1957	1957
26	22	4	17	22	4
1992	1988	1970	1974	1979	1961
26	26	8	17	26	8
2018	2014	1978	1991	2005	1969

1940	1940	1940
8	8	8
1948	1948	1948
8	22	4
1956	1970	1952
8	17	8
1964	1987	1960

EMOTIONAL—Universal Time

3. month   5

1940	1940	1940
5	5	5
1945	1945	1945
5	19	1
1950	1964	1946
5	20	2
1955	1984	1948

4. month + year   5+17=22/4; 5+8=13/4

1940	1940	1940	1940	1940	1940
22	22	22	13	13	13
1962	1962	1962	1953	1953	1953
22	18	9	13	18	9
1984	1980	1971	1966	1971	1962
22	18	9	13	18	9
2006	1998	1980	1979	1989	1971

1940	1940	1940
4	4	4
1944	1944	1944
4	18	9
1948	1962	1953
4	18	9
1952	1980	1962

SPIRITUAL—date of conception
1. year   1940=14/5

1940	1940	1940	1940	1940	1940
14	14	14	5	5	5
1954	1954	1954	1945	1945	1945
14	19	1	5	19	1
1968	1973	1955	1950	1964	1946
14	20	2	5	20	2
1982	1993	1957	1955	1984	1948

2. month+day+year   12+19+14=45/9;   12+19+5=36/9;   12+10+14=36/9;
                                            12+1+14=27/9;   3+19+14=36/9;   3+10+14=27/9;
                                            3+1+14=18/9; 3+1+5=9;   12+10+5=27/9;   12+10+5=27/9

Use 45, 36 (once), 27 (once), 18, and 9.

1940	1940	1940	1940	1940	1940
45	45	45	36	36	36
1985	1985	1985	1976	1976	1976
45	23	5	36	23	5
2030	2008	1990	2012	1999	1981
45	10	1	36	28	1
	2018	1991	2048	2027	1982

1940	1940	1940	1940	1940	1940
27	27	27	18	18	18
1967	1967	1967	1958	1958	1958
27	23	5	18	23	5
1994	1990	1972	1976	1981	1963
27	19	1	18	19	1
2021	2009	1973	1994	2000	1964

1940	1940	1940
9	9	9
1949	1949	1949
9	23	5
1958	1972	1954
9	19	1
1967	1991	1955

Breaking the Code

SPIRITUAL—Universal Time
3. year   17/8

1940	1940	1940	1940	1940	1940
17	17	17	8	8	8
1957	1957	1957	1948	1948	1948
17	22	4	8	22	4
1974	1979	1961	1956	1970	1952
17	26	8	8	17	8
1991	2005	1969	1964	1987	1960

4. month+day+year   5+19+17=41/5;   5+10+17=32/5;   5+1+17=23/5;
                         5+19+8=32/5;   5+10+8=23/5;   5+1+8=14/5 Use
41, 32, 23, 14, and 5 each once.

1940	1940	1940	1940	1940	1940
41	41	41	32	32	32
1981	1981	1981	1972	1972	1972
41	19	1	32	19	1
2022	2000	1982	2004	1991	1973
41	2	2	32	20	2
	2002	1984	2036	2011	1975

1940	1940	1940	1940	1940	1940
23	23	23	14	14	14
1963	1963	1963	1954	1954	1954
23	19	1	14	19	1
1986	1982	1964	1968	1973	1955
23	20	2	14	20	2
2009	2002	1966	1982	1993	1957

1940	1940	1940
5	5	5
1945	1945	1945
5	19	1
1950	1964	1946
5	20	2
1955	1984	1948

Be sure to take each of these columns to 100 +/-5 years.

Notice that these numbers also repeat for emphasis. They can also be charted on another of the same sets of charts at the end of chapter 9.

Chapter 11

YEARS IN A TRIANGLE

These years in the chart can be made into a triangle to show the relationship between each set of dots. Divide the triangle into 18 equal parts. This is one of the reasons that graph paper is convenient—the lines at the bottom can be divided into 18 parts. Label the bottom of the triangle physical, mental, emotional, and spiritual and add the number 1, 2, 3, 4 to each part. The middle 2 parts are the core of light of the person. The first 4 numbers are physical, the second 4 parts are mental, then the core of light. The next 4 parts are emotional, and the last 4 are spiritual.

The physical years are placed in the appropriate space, from hour and minute of birth, day and year of birth, and the Universal Time hour and minute, day and year.

The next four are placed in the mental body years and those dates important to our mental development.

Then skip two spaces (for the core of light). This is only 1/9 of the total triangle, but an extremely important part. This is the part of our being that may be called our essence, or spark of the Divine.

On the right of the core of light, we put the emotional years as found previously. Then the spiritual years are charted on the last four spaces.

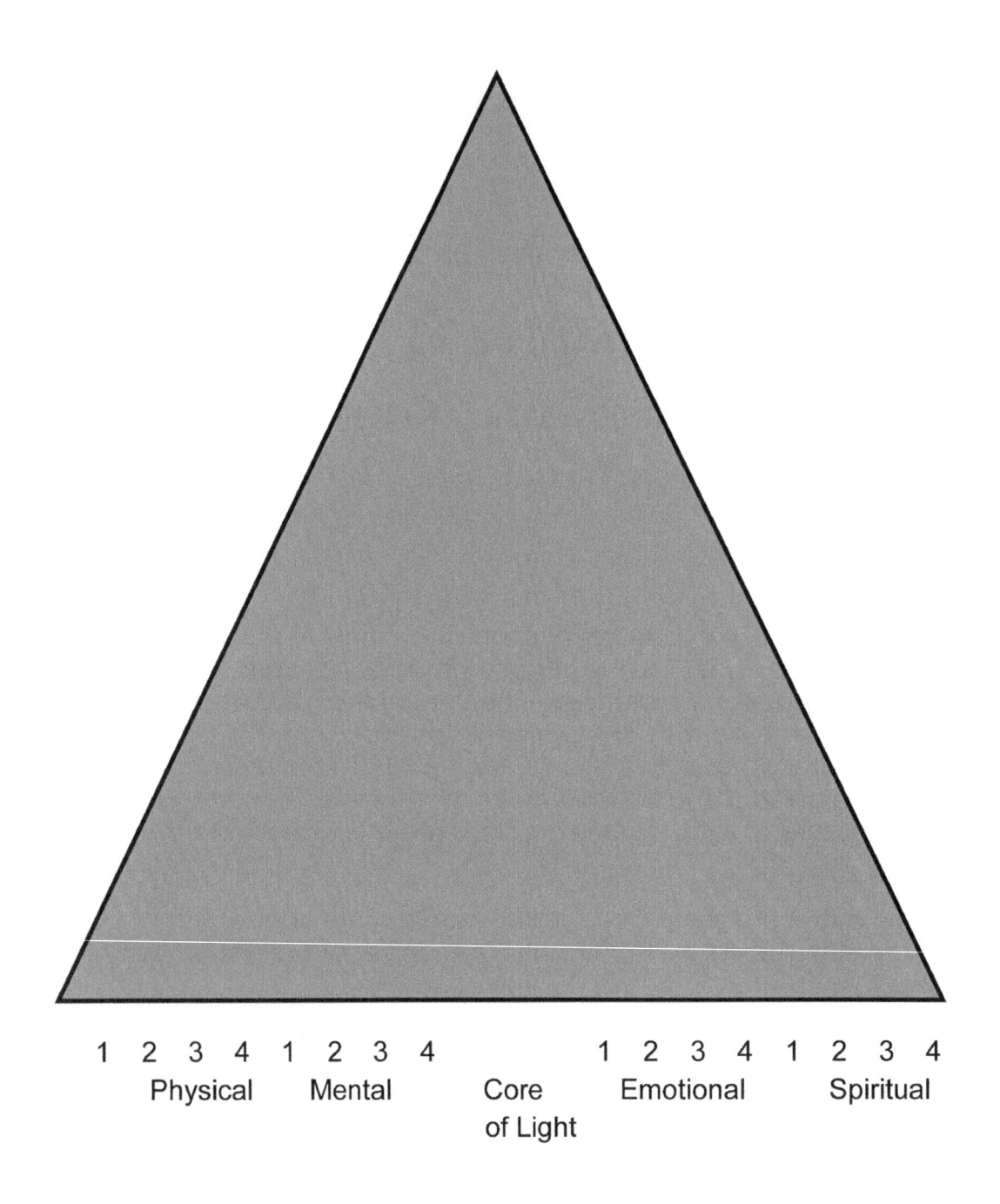

1 2 3 4	1 2 3 4		1 2 3 4	1 2 3 4
Physical	Mental	Core of Light	Emotional	Spiritual

Chapter 12

TIME LINE PATTERNS

The third chart takes the sequencing of years from 1900-2050, and plots all the important years by circling that specific year. Use different colors for physical, mental, emotional, and spiritual data. This will tell you quickly which sets of numbers are important at which time.

This set of charts is important in other ways, also. There are seven stems. One is composed of all the years that reduce to nine, one uses all the years reducing to three or six. The other five stems contain all the other numbers—but in the sequence 1, 2, 4, 8, 7, 5! Those with years adding to nine have the option of finishing a single lesson or completing work during this lifetime. Those with many threes and sixes are good with groups or in service connected areas. Those with many of the 1, 2, 4, 8, 7, 5 years (the majority of us) are working on those parts that need to be perfected. What we accomplish this life-time need not be repeated by another incarnation. We can go on to other lessons at that time.

These stems contain only the years 1900-2050. They can be used to find several different things. First, we can use these stems to find out our own patterns: are we using mainly the nine pattern, the three/six pattern, or the 1/2/4/8/7/5 pattern for our physical, mental, emotional and spiritual paths. All we need to do is to find the years that are important to us and chart them on this page. Use different colors for each set of years. I usually use red for physical, blue for mental, green for emotional, and purple for spiritual. Refer to previous chapters for information on how to find these years.

Second, we can use these stems to access information about our family and friends, using just their birth year. Chart the birth YEAR for your parents, spouse, children, and perhaps grandchildren. Some dates will be on the same stem, others will be on different stems. Sometimes children will be on even different stems. I have also found that these stem years can show you which path you are on and if you "belong" to your parental line or start off on your own. The same way, you can see how your family is connected (or not). For instance, I belong to the completed line of both my mother and father. One of my children belongs to the line of his stepfather, while the other child and two of his step-brothers and step-sister belong to the same line—different from either natural parent or me! Those that are on the same stems, or at least the same set (9, 3/6, 1/2/4/8/7/5) will find that they have more in common than those with different core stems. Many best friends will also be found on the same stem or same set of stems.

Another interesting pattern for these years is that 1500-2075 shows up as only five pathways. In 1840 there become six, and in 1919 become seven. By the year 2055, there are 11 pathways, with four of them starting in 2022 (six), 2033 (eight), 2944 (one), and 2055 (three). Then there will be three pathways of three/six numbers, one for the nines, and seven within the one-two-four-eight-seven-five series.

Each piece of the stem can, I believe, be shown to be part of the political world history. Each set of numbers is a related series of events concerning world events within a historical perspective. The years on your chart tell in which category (physical, mental, emotional, spiritual) those events will affect your life, according to where that particular dot is located. Each stem of years concerns one area of history or one field—religion, medicine, government, exploration, war, etc. Where the two numbers form a new line, something of great importance within this area has happened. The new line then indicates when this new wave was incorporated into society.

Using these charts, we find what can be called "hollow years"—those years that are a single digit, even after adding all the parts together. They are the years that pull together two other stems into one of the final seven stems. These include 2002, 2003, 2004, 2006, 2010, 2012, 2014, 2015, 2016, 2017. It also includes those numbers that are as high as you can get: 1997 (adds to 26), 1998 (adds to 27) and 1999 (adds to 28).

As you can see, this includes many of the years from 1987 to 2017, a thirty year period that would coincide with other psychic prophecies of hard times.

The years of the beginning of the eleven new stems are 2008, 2013, 2021, 2022, 2023, 2025, 2027, 2033, 2044, 2055, 2064. By this time, the world will be back to normal for that age and will not change again for many, many years.

There seems to be years of trouble, rest, then trouble, then rest in the following pattern: 1997, 1998, 1999, 2000, 2001-2003, 2004, 2005-2009, 2010, 2011, 2012-2015, 2016, 2017.

The years 2010-2015 seem to have something to do with space and/or UFOs. If any of these dates are in your important years, you seem to have the opportunity to be involved with space beings. If you do not have these numbers, it does not mean you cannot, but it will be through a different method or means.

The dates 2010-2011 seem to involve Canada and North; 2013-2014 the United States, Mexico and Central America; 2015-2017 South America and South.

I have some ideas about the historical framework of these stems, but it is not relevant to this book at this time.

Use the year chart on the following page to plot the important years for you and your family.

YEARS 1900 TO 2050

```
         2052        2048      2054         2049
         2043        2041      2044         2037
         2034        2033                   2031
         2025                               2019
      //////\/\\\\\                      //////\\\\\\\
   1998      2016                        2013       1995
   1980       ///\\                   /////\\\\\\\  1974
   1962    2007    1989                2010    1992
   1944       1971                  /////\\\\\\\ 1968    2057
   1926       1953              2004        1986  1947   2046
   1908       1935             //\\\\\\\    1965  1932   2040
              1917        1983    2001 1950 1920         2028
                          1959    1977 1929 1905         2022
                   2051   1936    1956 1914
                   2038   1923    1941 1902
                   2027   1911
              ////////\\\\\\\\\\\\                       2055
              2017         1989    2050
        /////////  ////\\\\\\\\    1976    2029
    2012          1994     1960    2018
    //\\\\         1969    1943    2008
 1987 2005         1952    1930     // \\          2047
 1970 1979                      1985  2003         2036
 1948 1957                            1978         2026
 1928 1937    2045        2053        1961         2021
 1909 1918    2035        2039        1939         //\\\\
      1904    2030        2034        1919    2014     1996
              2023        2024          1988 //\\ 2006
              //\\\        2020          1966   /\\\\\\\\\\
         2015    1997      2009       1946 1982       2002
          //\\\  1975      1990       1927 1964       /// \\
       2011 1993 1955      1967       1913 1945   2000   1982
       1991 1973 1936      1951            1931   1981   1963
       1972 1954 1922      1934            1915   1958
       1949 1940 1906      1921                   1942
       1933 1924            1910                  1925
       1916 1907            1900                  1912
       1903                                       1901
```

82 *Donna Linn*

Chapter 13

THE NINES PATTERN

Using the calendar years from 1 A. D. to 4000 A. D., I have found strands of years that go together in a pattern. There are three different sets of these numbers. The next three chapters shows these patterns: chapter 13 explains the nines, chapter 14 the threes and sixes, and chapter 15 continues the pattern of the rest of the years (1-2-4-8-7-5).

These stems also make patterns through the centuries. I believe each of these stems belongs to new ideas of the time in different areas—health, science, literature, economics, government, etc.

The years are related through century and through related stem years. These three chapters first show the pattern of the stems and then the relationships between the centuries.

CHART OF NINES

```
    9                              612
   18                              621
   27                              630
   36                              639    648
   45                              657    666
   54                              675    684
   63                              693    702
   72                                \\V//
   81                               711
   90                               720
   99        108                    729
     \\\V///                        747    738
    117                             765    756
    126                             783    774
    135                             801    792
    144                               \\V//
    153                              810
    162                              819    828
    171                              837    846
    180                              855    864
    189                              873    882
    207      198                    891    900
      \V/                              \\\V///    918
     216                               909        936
     225                               927        954
     234                               945        972
     243                               963        990
     252                               981       1008
     261                               999       1017
     270                                 \V/
     279      288                      1026
     297      306                      1035
       \\\V///                         1044
      315                              1053
      324                              1062
      333                              1071
      342                              1080
      351                              1089
      360                             1107      1098
      369                                \\V//
378   387                             1116
369   405                             1125
  \\\V//////                          1134
    414                               1143
    423                               1152
    432                               1161
    441                               1170
    450                              1179      1188
    459     488                      1197      1206
    477     486                         \\V//
    495     504                       1215
        \V/                           1224
       513                            1233
       522                            1242
       531                            1251
       540                            1260
       549                            1269
       567     558                   1287     1278
       585     576                   1305     1296
       603     594                      \\V//
          \V/--612  ↑                   1314            →
```

84 *Donna Linn*

```
1314                                              2115
1323                                              2124
1332                                              2133
1341                                              2142
1350                                              2151
1359    1368                                      2160
1377    1386                                      2169
1395    1404                                      2187    2178
   \\V//                                          2205    2196
   1413                                              \\V//
   1422                                              2214
   1431                                              2223
   1440                                              2232
   1449                                              2241
   1467    1458                                      2250
   1485    1476                                      2259    2268
   1503    1494                                      2277    2286
      \\V///                                         2295    2304
      1502                                              \\V//
      1521                                              2313
      1530                                              2322
      1539    1548                                      2331
      1557    1566                                      2340
      1576    1584                                      2349
      1593    1602                                      2367    2358
         \\V//                                          2385    2376
         1611                                           2403    2394
         1620                                              \V/
         1629                                              2412
         1647    1636                                      2421
         1665    1656                                      2430
         1683    1674                                      2439    2448
         1701    1692                                      2457    2466
            V                                             2475    2484
            1710                                          2493    2502
            1719    1728                                     \\V//
            1737    1748                                     2511
            1755    1764                                     2520
            1773    1782                                     2529
            1791    1800                                     2547    2538
               \\V//                                         2565    2556
               1809    1818                                  2583    2574
               1827    1836                                  2601    2592
               1845    1854                                     \\V//
               1863    1872                                     2610
               1881    1890                                     2619    2628
      1917     1899    1908                                     2637    2646
      1935        \\V//                                         2655    2664
      1953        1926                                          2673    2682
      1971        1944                                          2691    2700
      1989  2007  1962                                             \\V//
         \V/     1980                                              2709    2718
         2016    1998                                              2727    2736
            \\V///                                                 2745    2754
            2025                                                   2763    2772
            2034                                                   2781    2790
            2043                                                   2799    2808
            2052                                                      \\V//
            2061                                                      2826   →
            2070
      2088    2079
      2106 V  2097V2115 ↑
```

Breaking the Code 85

```
        2826                                3510
        2844            2817                3519    3528
        2862            2835                3537    3546
        2880            2853                3555    3564
        2898    2907    2871                3575    3582
           \\V//        2889                3591    3600
                2925    2916                   \V/
                2943    2934                        3609    3618
                2961    2952                        3627    3636
                2979    2970                        3645    3654
                3006    2988                        3663    3672
                  \\\\V/////                        3681    3690
        2997            3015                        3699    3708
          \\\\V/////                                    \V/
                3024                                    3726
                3033                                    3744
                3042                                    3762
                3051                                    3780
                3060                        3807    3798        3717
                3069                           \V/              3735
                3087    3078                    3825            3753
                3105    3096                    3843            3771
                   \\V//                         3861            3789
                   3114                          3879            3816
                   3123                 3897    3906            3894
                   3132                          V              3852
                   3141                        3924             3870
                   3150                        3942             3888
                   3159    3168                3960             3915
                   3177    3166                3978             3933
                   3195    3204        3987    4005             3951
                      \V/                  \\V//                3969
                      3213                4014                  3996
                      3222                   \\\\\\\\V/////////////
                      3231                                4023
                      3240
                      3249
                      3267    3258
                      3285    3276
                      3303    3294
                         \V/
                         3401
                         3420
                         3429
                         3447    3438
                         3465    3456
                         3482    3474
                         3501    3492
                            \\V//
                            3510   ↑
```

86 *Donna Linn*

The nines follow a pattern for the strings of years filtering into the main pattern. These are end-of-cycle years because all years can be reduced to either 9, 18, or 27. From the year 108 to the very late 3000s, there is a distinct pattern similar with each thousand years. This is shown by the following chart. As you can see, there are two anomalies—seven years (not six) in the 918-1017 string and one year (not two) at the year 2997.

Notice too, how the same numbers repeat from each thousand years. The years 100-1017 correlate with 2000-2808. The first two as single years, but starting with the two year strands, the ending two years are the same while the first two years add to the same number. The same things happen with the years 2000s and 3000s. The first anomaly suggested previously is not really—the seven has the 1017 that progresses to 1917—then adds five more at 2817 and five more at 3717.

I believe that each set of years can recap what went before with that same number. Someone will come up with the precise challenges for precise years. I have some ideas, but they do not fit within the scope of this book.

There is also a double entry on each side of the 2000s, 3000s, and 4000s. See the years 2016, 3015, and 4014. There is none in the 1000s, although by pattern it should be the year 1017

Even though all these years reduce to nine, some of them first reduce to 18 and a few reduce to nine from 27. All of these are end-of-cycle years, perhaps a final check as to whether we have learned the lesson of the original—i.e., 108—self plus power, 1989—self plus power plus two end-of-cycle nines. Those that reduce to only nine seems to be physical endings, while 18 to mental and emotional endings. The twenty seven uses balance and spirituality for spiritual endings.

The chart that follows shows the patterns I have found within the nines numbers:

    1—patterns of years for stems 1 to approximately 1000
    2—patterns of years for stems approximately 1000 to approximately 2000
    3—patterns of years for stems approximately 2000 to approximately 3000
    4—patterns of years for stems approximately 3000 to approximately 4000

Each set of years corresponds to the 1 or the 1-1-2-2-3-3-4-4-5-5-6-X pattern. They are as follows for each thousand years (1-1000, 1000-2000, 2000-3000, 3000-4000).

Breaking the Code 87

1	1	2	2	3	3	4	4	5	6	X
108	198	288	378	468	558	648	758	828	918	
	306	396	486	576	666	756	846	936		
		504	594	684	774	864	954			
					702	792	882	975		
							900	990		
								1008		
								1017		
	1098	1188	1278	1458	1548	1638	1728	1818	1917	
		1206	1296	1386	1476	1566	1656	1746	1836	1935
				1404	1494	1584	1674	1764	1854	1953
						1602	1692	1782	1872	1971
								1800	1880	1989
									1908	
2007		2088	2178	2268	2358	2448	2538	2628	2718	2817
		2106	2196	2286	2376	2466	2556	2646	2736	2835
				2304	2394	2484	2574	2664	2754	2853
						2502	2592	2682	2772	2871
								2700	2797	2889
									2808	2916
										2934
										2952
										2970
										2988
2907	2997		3078	3168	3258	3348	3438	3528	3618	3717
			3096	3186	3276	3366	3456	3546	3636	3735
				3204	3294	3354	3474	3564	3654	3753
						3402	3492	3582	3672	3771
								3600	3690	3789
									3708	3816
										3834
										3852
										3870
										3888
										3915
										3933
										3951
										3969
										3996
3007	3897	3987								

There is another way to look at this table. See how the numbers are the same in each thousand years. The only changes are within the first two year-numbers which shows which thousand years we are talking about.

Patterns of 2
288-306
1188-1206
2008-2106

379-396
1278-1296
2178-2196
3078-3096

Patterns of 3
468-486-504
1368-1386-1404
2268-2286-2304
3168-3186-3204

558-576-594
1458-1476-1494
2358-2376-2394
3258-3276-3294

Patterns of 4
648-666-684-702
1548-1566-1584-1602
2448-2466-2484-2502
3348-3366-3384-3402

738-756-774-792
1638-1656-1674-1692
2538-2556-2574-2562
3438-3456-3474-3492

Patterns of 5
828-846-864-882-900
1728-1746-1764-1782-1800
2628-2646-2864-2682-2700
3526-3546-3564-3582-3600

1917-1932-1953-1971-1989
see odd pattern explanation

Patterns of 6
918-936-954-972-990-1008
1818-1836-1854-1872-1890-1908
2718-2736-2754-2772-2790-2808
3618-3636-3854-3672-3690-3708

Odd pattern of 5, then 10, then 15
1917-1935-1953-1971-1989
2817-2835-2853-2871-2889-2916-2934-2952-9270-2988
3717-3753-3771-3789-3816-3834-3852-3870-3888-3915-3933-3951-3969-3996

The year 1017 is an oddity, because it is a continuation of another stem instead of beginning its own pattern. Therefore, the odd pattern does not start until 1917.

Breaking the Code 89

Single beginnings of stems

108   198   2007 2907 2997 3987
      1098   3907 3897

Bringing two stems together into a third stem

2016
3015
4014

    Another way to look at the stems for each century is as follows: look to see how the pattern is so consistent—changing only one number each century--1+7, 1+7, 1+7, 1+7, 7+1.

Stems—similar within each century

288	1188	2088	
378	1278	2178	3078
468	1368	2268	3168
558	1458	2358	3258
648	1548	2448	3348
738	1638	2538	3438
828	1728	2628	3528
918	1818	2718	3618
1+7	1+7	1+7	7

90 *Donna Linn*

Chapter 14
THE THREE/SIX PATTERN

```
                        3                                           210
                        6                                           213    222
                       12                                           219    228
                       15                                           231    240
                       21                                           237    246
                       24                                           249    258
                       30      42                                   264    273
                       33      28                            255    276    285
                       39      60                            267    291    300
                       51      66     75                     282       \\\ ///
                       57      78     87                     294         303
                       69      93    102             312        \\\ ///
                       84        \\ //               318        309
                       96         105                330        321
                          \\\\\\\ ///////            336        327
                              111                    348        339
                              114                    363        354
                              120                    375        366          345
                              123                    390        381          357
                              129                    402        393          372
                              141                           \\/              384
        132                   147                           408              399
        158                   159                              \\ //
        150     165           174                              420 (a)
        156     177           186
        168     192           201
        183        \\\\///
        195         204
           \\\\\\\///////
               210  ↑
```

```
                420
                426    411
                438    417    435
                453    429    447
                465    444    462
                480    456    474
        501     492    471    489
          \\\ ///      483    510             525
            507              498    516             537
                  \\\ ///    528             552
                519          543             564
                534          555             579
                546          570    591    600                      615
                561          582      \\ //                         627
                573          597          606                       642
                588               \\\ ///                            654
                609                 618                             669
                624                 633                  681        690
                636                 645                  696        705
                651                 660                        \\ //
                663                 672                        717
                678                 687                        732
                699                 708                        744
                    \\\\\\    //////                           759
                        723                                    780
                        735                         804        795
                        750                                \\ //
                771     765                                    816
        714     786     777                                    831
        726     807     798                                    843
        741       \\\ ///                                      858
        753          822                                       879
        768          834                               894     903
        789          849                                 \\ //
        813          870    861                             915
        825          885    876                             930
        840          906    897                             942
        852            \\\\ ////                             957
        867             921                                  978
        888             933          951       984    1002
        912             948          966         \\ //
        924             969          987              1005
        939             993             \\\\\  /////
        960              \\\\\\\\              1011
        975               \\\\\\\\\  /////////////
        996                        1014
        \\\\\\\\\\\\\\\\\\\\V///////////////////
                         1020   (b)
```

92 *Donna Linn*

```
                1020→ 1023   (a)                                    b
                      1029
                      1041
                      1047   1032
                      1059   1038
                1065  1074   1050
                1077  1086   1056
                1092  1101   1068
                       \\ //  1083
                       1104   1095
                      \\\\ //////////////
                       1110
                       1113   1122
                       1119   1128
                       1131   1140
                       1137   1146
                       1149   1158
                       1164   1173
                       1176   1185   1155
                       1191   1200   1167
                          \\\ ///    1182
                          1203       1194
                1212          \\\ ///
                1218          1209
                1230          1221
                1236          1227
                1248          1239
                1263          1254
         1245   1275          1266
         1257   1290          1281
         1272   1302          1293
         1264          \\\V///
         1299          1308
            \\\\ ////
             1320
             1326   1311
             1338   1317                 1335
             1353   1329                 1347
             1365   1344                 1362
             1368   1356                 1374
      1401   1392   1371                 1389
        \\ //       1383          1425   1410
        1407        1398          1437   1416
       \\\\\ /////                1452   1428
             1419                 1464   1443
             1434                 1479   1455
             1446         1491    1500   1470
          1461-1473              \\ // 1506   1482-1497  (c)
```

Breaking the Code 93

```
1473        1497(c)    1506                                    c
1488          ////\\\\\\      1515                           c
1509           1518      1527
1524           1533      1542
1536           1545      1554
1551           1560      1569
1563           1572  1581  1590
1578           1578  1596  1605
1599           1608      ///\\\\
       \\V///            1617
        1623             1635
        1635             1644
        1650             1659
1671    1662             1680
1686    1677   1704      1695                          1614
1707    1698      \\\\V////                            1625
  \\\V///           1716                               1641
        1722        1731                               1653
        1734        1743                               1666
        1748        1758                               1689
1761    1770        1779                               1713
1776    1785   1794  1803                              1725
1797    1806      \\V////                              1740
  \\\V///           1815                               1752
   1821             1830                               1767
   1833             1842                               1788
   1848             1857        1851                   1812
   1869             1878        1866                   1824
   1893             1902        1887                   1839
       \\\\\\V////////           1911                   1860
          \V/         1941      1923    1884   1875
           1914       1956      1938    1905   1896
           1929       1977      1959      \\\V////
           1950       2001      1963       1920
           1965    \\\\\\\V//////           1932
           1986         2004                1947
            \\\\\\\\\\V/////////            1968
                  2010                      1992
          \\\\\\\\\\\\\\\V////////////           1974
                    2013                         1995
              \\\\\\\\\\\V////////////
                         2019 (d)
```

94 *Donna Linn*

```
                    2022                                                    d
                    2028            2019 c
                    2040            2031
                    2046            2038
                    2058            2049
                    2073            2064
        2055        2085            2076
        2067        2100            2091
        2082                \\\\  ////
        2094              2103
2112                \\\  ///
2118                2109
2130                2121
2136                2127
2148                2139
2163                2154
2175                2166     2145
2190                2181     2157
2202                2193     2172
    \\\\  ////               2184
        2208                 2199
                    \\\  ///
                    2220
                    2226     2211
                    2238     2217                    2235
                    2253     2229                    2247
                    2265     2244                    2262
                    2280     2256                    2274
        2301        2292     2271                    2289
            \\  //           2283          2325      2310
            2307             2298          2337      2318
            \\\\  ////                     2352      2328
                    2319                   2364      2343
                    2334                   2379      2355
                    2346          2391     2400      2370
                    2361            \\\  ///         2382
                    2373           2406              2397
                    2388            \\\\  ////                2415
                    2409                   2418               2427
                    2424                   2433               2442
                    2436                   2445               2454
                    2451                   2460               2469
                    2463                   2472       2481    2490
                    2478                   2487       2496    2505
                    2499                   2508              \\  //
                        \\\\\\\\\\  //////////                2517  (e)
                            2523   (e)
```

```
2514                                                                2517 (d)      e
2526                                          2523  (d)             2532
2541                                          2535                  2544
2553                                          2550                  2559
2568                              2571        2562                  2580
2599                              2586        2577        2604      2595
2613                              2807        2598                  \\ //
2625                                      \\ //                     2616
2640                                          2622                  2631
2652                                          2634                  2643
2667                                          2649                  2658
2688                              2661        2670                  2679
2712                              2676        2688        2694      2703
2724                              2697        2706                  \\\ ///
2738                                      \\\ ///                   2715
2760                                          2721                  2730
2775              2784                        2733        2742      2751
2796              2805                        2748        2757      2766
         \\\\\\\  ///////                     2769        2778      2787
              2820                            2793        2802      2811
2814     2832                             \\\\\\\\\\\  ///////////  2823
2856     2847                                 2814                  2838
2877     2868                                 2828                  2859
2901     2892                                 2850        2874      2883
         \\\ ///                              2865        2895      2904
   2913     2931                              2886                  \\ //
   2928     2946                              2910                  2919
   2949     2967                              2922                  2940
   2973     2991                              2937                  2965
   2994     3012                              2958                  2976
         \\\\ ///                             2982                  3000
          3018  (f)                 2964              \\\\\\\\\  /////////
                                       2985        3003
                                             \\\\\\\  ////////
                                              3009  (f)
```

96 *Donna Linn*

3018 (e)	3009 (e)						f
3030	3021						
3036	3027						
3048	3039						
3036	3054						
3075	3066	3056					
3090	3081	3057					
3102	3093	3072					
\\\ ///		3084					
3108		3099					
	\\\ ////						
	3120						
	3126	3111					
	3138	3117	3136				
	3153	3129	3147				
	3165	3144	3162				
	3180	3156	3174				
3201	3092	3071	3089				
\\\ ///		3183	3210		3225		
3207		3198	3216		3237		
\\\\ \ /////			3228		3252		
3219			3243		3264		
3234			3255		3279		
3246			3270	3291	3300		
3261			3282		\\ //		
3273			3297		3306		
3288			\\\ ////			3315	
3309			3318			3327	
3324			3333			3342	
3336			3345			3354	
3351			3360			3369	3381
3363			3372			3390	3381
3378			3387			3405	3306
3399			3408			\\\ ///	
\\\ /////						3417	
3432						3432	
3435						3444	
3450						3459	
3462			3471			3480	
3477			3486		3504	3495	
3398			3507			\\\ //	
\\\\\\\\\\\\ ////////////						3516 (g)	
3522 (g)							

Breaking the Code 97

  g

                                                                              3414
                                                                              3426
                                                                              3441
                                                                              3453
                                                                              3468
                                                                              3499
                                              3516   (f)   3513
                    (f)   3522   3531   3525
                          3534   3543   3540
                          3549   3558   3552
    3561   3570   3579   3567   3567
    3576   3585   3603   3594   3588
    3597   3606   \\\ ///   3612
           \\\\\\ /////   3615   3624
           3621   3630   3639
           3633   3642   3660
           3648   3657   3684   3675
           3669   3678   3705   3696
           3693   3702   \\\ ///
                  \\\\\\\\\ //////////   3720
                          3714   3741   3732
                          3729   3756   3747
                          3750   3768   3777
                          3765   3777   3768
                          3786   3801   3792
                          3810   \\\\\ /////
                          3822   3813
                          3837   3828
                          3868   3849
                          3882   3873
                          3903   3894
                  3921   \\\\\\\\\\\\ ////////////
                  3936   3918
                  3957   3939
                  3981   3963
                  4002   3984
                         \\\\\\\\\\\\\\ //////////////
                                4008

98 *Donna Linn*

```
                    3651
                    3666
                    3687
                    3711
                    3723
                    3738
                    3759
                    3783            3774
                    3804            3796
                       \\\\\\\ ///////
                       3819
                       3840            3831
                       3855            3848
            3864       3876            3867
            3885       3900            3891
            3909           \\\\\\\ ///////
            3930       3912
            3945       3927
            3966       3948
            3990       3972
            4011       3993            3954
           \\\\\\\\\\ //////////////    3975
               4017                     3999
                   \\\\\\\\\\\\\\\\V///////////////
                           4029
```

The strands that reduce to three or six (including 12, 15, and 24) are also very interesting.. This pattern is totally different from the nine pattern. Connecting two strands to the main strand is shown in the following chart.

```
105   111   210    309   420   519   618   717   723   616   822   915
      1011  1110   1209  1320  1419  1518  1617  1623  1716  1722  1815
            2010no 2109  2220  2319  2418  2517  2523  2616  2622  2715
                   3009  3120  3219  3318  3417  3423  3516  3522  3615

921   1020  1914   2019  2913  3018  3912
1821  1920  2814   2919  3813  3918
2721  2820  3714   3819
3621  3720
```

Breaking the Code 99

Another way to write these strands to give an indication of the myriad patterns within the years of our centuries is as follows.

105			
111	1011		
210	1110		
309	1309	2109	3009
420	1320	2220	3120
519	1419	2319	3219
618	1518	2418	3318
717	1617	2517	3417
723	1623	2523	3423
816	1716	2616	3516
822	1722	2622	3522
915	1915	2715	3615
921	1921	2721	3621
1020	1920	2820	3720
	1914	2814	3714
	2019	2119	3819
		2913	3813
		3018	3918
		3912	

The first column is 1+2+11=14, the second is 2+11+2+=15. The third column is 11+2+2=15, while the fourth column is 11+2+2+1=16

Then there are single strands that bring two separate strands into a third strand. This happens once each century. In the 1000s the years are 1005, 1011, 1014. In the 2000s these years are 2004, 2010 and 2013. But in the 3000s there is only 3003, not as we would expect 3009 or 3012

Another way to follow the strands includes how many years are in the stem. I have charted strings of 1, 2, 3, 4, 5, 6, 8, 13, and 18 years as follows.

Patterns of 1
501-591   804-894   984-continued in twos
1401-1491   1704-1794
2301-2391   2604-2694
3201-3291   3504-3594

Patterns of 2
681-696
1581-1596   1884-1905   1974-1995
2481-2496   2784-2805   2874-2895   2964-2985
3381-3396   3684-3905   3774-3795   3864-not

100 *Donna Linn*

Patterns of 3
75-87-102   165-177-192   3954-3975-3999
                                   1056-1077-1092

771-786-807   861-876-897
1671-1686-1707   1761-1776-1797
2571-2586-2607   2661-2676-2697
3471-3486-3507   3561-3576-3597

Patterns of 3, but continue on for 8 and 9 more numbers
951-966-987
1851-1866-1887-1911-1923-1938-1959-1983
2751-2766-2787-2811-2823-2838-2859-2883-2904
3651-3666-3687-3711-3723-3738-3759-3783-3804

Patterns of 4
255-267-282-294   1941-1956-1977-2001   3831-3846-3867-3891
1155-1167-1182-1194   2841-2856-2877-2901
2055-2067-2082-2094   3741-3756-3777-3801

Patterns of 5
345-357-372-384-399   3921-3936-3957-3981-4002
1245-1257-1272-1284-1299
2145-2157-2172-2184-2199
3045-3057-3072-3084-3099

2931-2946-2967-2991-3012
3831-3846-3867-3911

Patterns of 6
42-48-60-66-78-93

525-537-552-564-579-600
1425-1437-1452-1464-1479-1500
2325-2337-2352-2364-2379-2400
3225-3237-3252-3264-3279-3300

Patterns of 7
132-138-150-156-168-183-195   417—see eights for continuation
1032-1038-1050-1056-1068-1083-1095

615-627-642-654-669-690-705
1515-1527-1542-1554-1569-1590-1605
2415-2427-2442-2454-2469-2490-2505
3315-3327-3342-3354-3369-3390-3405

Breaking the Code 101

Patterns of 8
222-228-240-246-258-273-285-300
1122-1128-1140-1146-1158-1173-1185-1200
2022-2028-2040-2046-2058-2073-2085-2100

417-429-444-456-471-483-498
1311-1317-1329-1344-1356-1371-1383-1398
2200-2217-2229-2244-2258-2271-2283-2298
3111-3117-3129-3144-3156-3171-3183-3198

3864-3885-3909-3930-3945-3966-3990-4011

Patterns of 9
312-318-330-336-348-362-375-390-402
1212-1218-1230-1236-1248-1262-1275-1290-1302
2112-2118-2130-2136-2148-2162-2175-2190-2202
3012 not

Patterns of 13
435-437-462-474-489-510-516-528-543-555-570-582-597
1335-1347-1362-1374-1398-1410-1416-1428-1443-1455-1470-1482-1497
2235-2247-2262-2274-2289-2310-2316-2328-2343-2355-2370-2382-2397

Patterns of 18
714-726-741-753-768-789-813-825-840-852-867-888-912-924-939-960-975-996
1614-1626-1641-1653-1668-1689-1713-1725-1740-1752-1767-1788-1812-1824-1839-
1860-1875-1896

2514-2526-2541-2553-2568-2589-2613-2625-2640-2652-2667-2688-2712-2724-2739-
2760-2775-2796

3414-3426-3441-3453-3468-3489-3513-3525-3540-3552-3567-3588-3612-3624-3639-
3660-3675-3696

Another way to chart these patterns is as follows:

Ones
501   591   804   894
1401   1491   2391   3291
804   1704   2804   3504
894   1794   2694   3594
Four stems in each century

Twos
 681
1581 1884 1974
2481 2784 2874 2964
3381 3684 3774
4   3   3   1
Stems for each century

Threes
75   771 861 961
165 1671 1716
1065 2571 2661
     3471 3561
3   4   4   1
Stems for each century

Fours
255
1155 1941
2055 2841
     3741 3831
3   3   1
Stems for each century

Fives
345
1245
2145 2931
3045 3831 3921
4   2   1
Stems for each century

Sixes
42   525
     1425
     2325
     3225
1   4

Sevens
132 615
1032 1515
     2415
     3315
2   4

Eights
222 411
1122 1311 1815
2022 2211
     3111   3864
3   4   1   1
stems for each century

Nines
      312
1212
2112 2751
     3651
3   2
stems for each century

Thirteens
435
1335
2235
3136
4

Eighteens
714
1614
2514
3414
4

Breaking the Code 103

Chapter 15
PATTERN OF ONE-TWO-FOUR-EIGHT-SEVEN-FIVE

```
1                                                                               a
2
4
8
16
23
28                      7
38                     14
49                     19                                          5
62                     29                          31             10
70           53        40                          35             11   20
77    86     61        44                          43             13   22
91    100    68        52                          50             17   26
    \\\ ///  82        59                          55             25   34
      101    92        73                          65             32   41
         \\\\ /////    83    64                    76             37   46
101   103              94    74                    89             47   56
112       \\\\\\\\ /////////  85                  106    97       58   67
116              107         98                      \\\V///      71   80
124              \\\\\\\\\\ /////////                113          79   88
131                    115                           118          95  104
136                    122                           128             \\ //
146                    127                           139              109
157                    137                           152              119
170                    148                           160       143    130
178   187              161                   176     167       151    134
194   203              169                   190     181       158    142
    \\\\ ////          186                   200     191       172    149
      208              199                       \\\\\\\ //////  182  163
       \\\\\\\\\\\\\\\\ ////////////////          202          193    174
                  218                                \\\\\\\\ /////   184
                  229                                   206           197
                  242                                        \\\\ /////
                  250 (b)                                      214 (b)
```

```
233     250 (a)              209                 211                                  b
241     257     266          220                 215
248     271     280          224                 223
262     281     290          232                 230           214 (a)
272     292     301          239                 235           221
283         \\\ ///          253     244         245           226
296         305              263     254         256           236
     \\\\\ //////            274     265         269           247
            313              287     278     277 286           260
            320              304     295     293 302           268
            325     334           \\ //           \\ //        284
            335     344            311             307         298
            346     355            316             \\\\\\\\\\ //////////
            359     368            326                     317
            376     385            337                     328
367         392     401            350                     341
383         \\\ ///               358                     349
397             406                374                     365
     \\\\\ //////                  388                     379
            416                    407                     398
            427                    \\\\\\\\\\\\\\\ //////////////////
            440                            418
457         448                            431
473         464                            439
487         478                            455
506         497                            469
     \\\ ///                               488         479
     517                                   508         499
     530                                   \\\\\\\\ ////////
     538                                        521
     554                                        529
     568                                        546
     587                                        559
     607                                        578
  \\\\\\\\\\\\\\\\\\\\\\\\\\\\\\\            598
            //////////////////////////////////////
            620                    569
            628     637            589
            644     653            611
            658     667            619
            677     686            63 5
            697     706            649
            \\\ ///                668
            719   (c)              688     710
                                       \\\ ///
                                       718 (c)
```

106 *Donna Linn*

```
719 (b)                                                      c
736     727           718 (b)
755     757           734
785     776           748
805     796           767
   \\\ ///            787
   818                809
   835                826
   851                842
   865                856
   884                875
   904                895
        \\\\\\\\\ /////////////
              917
              934
              950
              964
              983           1001
              \\\\\\\\\\V/////////
                    1003 (f)
121
125
133
140
145         154
155         164
166         175
179         188
196         205
   \\\\\\\\ /////////
      212
      217
      227
      238
      251
      259
      275
      289
      308           299
         \\\\\\\\\\\V///////
              319 (d)
```

```
319 (c)                                                                    d
332                    310
340         356   323  314
347         370   331  322
361         380   338  329
371   400   391   352  343
382        \\\ ///  362  353
395        400    373  364         389
     \\\\\\ //////     386  377    409
           412        400  394    422   413
           419            \\\ ///   439   421
           433   424   410         437   428
           443   434   415         421   442
           454   445   425         461   452
           467   458   436         472   463
           484   475   449         485   476
           500   491   466         502   493
               \\\ ///     482            \\\ ///
                505        496            509
                     \\\\\\\\\ /////////      514   523
                          515              524   533
                          526              535   544
                          539              548   557
           547   556              565   574
           563   572              581   590
           577   586              595   604
           596   605                   \\\\\\ ////          613
              \\\\\\ //////               614              623
                   616                    625              634
                   629                    638              647
                   646                    655              664
                   662                    671              680
                   678                    685    703       694
                   695                    704       \\\ ///
                        \\\\\\\\\\\\\\\\\\\\\ /////////////////////        713                       716
                                  715                      724                                      730
                                  728                      737        760                           740
                        745                       754          773            764                   751
                                  761                      770        790                           781
                                  775                      784        806                           797
                                  794                      803                 \\\\\\\\\\ ///////
                                  \\\\\\\\\\\\\\\\\\\\\ /////////////////////           820
                                            814                                 830
                                            827                                 841
                                            844                                 854
                                            860                                 871
                                            874   883                           887
                                            893   902                           910
                                              \\\ ////                          920
                                               913 (f)                          931 (f)
                                               926                              944
```

```
446                                                                      e
460
470
481         490
494         503            512
 \\\\\\V///////             520
      511        536       527
      518        550       541
      532        560       551
      542        571       562
      553        584       575          580
      566        601       592    602   593
      583             \\\ ///      \\\ ///
      599             608       610           626
       \\\\\\\V//////////       617           640
            622                 631           650
            632                 641     670   661
            643                 652     683   674
            656                 665     700   691
            673                 682        \\\ ///
            689                 698        707
            712                  \\\\\\V////////                    659
            722                 721                                 679
            733                 731                692              701
            746                 742                \\\\\\\\V/////////
            763                 755                      709
            779                 772                      725
            802        793      788                      739
        \\\\\\\\V/////////      811            749       759
              812               821            769       778
              823               832            791       800
              836               845      782     \\\ ///
              853               862      799      808
              869               878   817    \\\\\\ ////
              892               901   833       824
         \\\\\\\\\\\V////////////   847     838              815
                    911             866     857              829
                    922             886     877        839   848
                    935             908     899        859   868
                    952              \\\\\\\V///////   881   890
                    968                   925          898   907
                    991    973            941            \\\ ////
                   1010    992             955           923
                       \\V//               974           937
                       1012                994           956
                 \\\\\\\\\\\\\V///////////////           976
                          1016                           998
                      \\\\\\\\\\\\\\\\\V/////////////////////
                                 1024  (f)
```

```
                                    926 (d)     944 (d)                              f
                                    943         961
850                                 959         977
863              872    916         982         1000
880              889    932         \\\\\\\\\V/////////
896    905       914    946    983              1001
\\V//            928    965         \\\\\\\\\\\\\\V/////////
       919       947    985              1003 (c)
       938       967         \\\\\\\\\\\\\\\V//////////
       958       989         107
       980           \\\\\\\\\\\V/////////     929
       997                 1015     (e) 1024   929          940
       \\\\\\\\\\\\\\\V//////////       1031   949          953              962
                        1022            1036   971          970              979
                        1027            1046   988          986              1004
                        1037            1057   1113   995   \\\\\\\\\\\V/////////
                        1048            1070        \\\V//                   1009
                        1061       1087 1078        1018                     1019
                        1069       1103 1094        1028   1043              1030
                        1085            \\\V//      1039   1051              1034
                        1099            1108        1052   1058    1076      1042
                   \\\\\\\\\\\V/////////            1060   1072    1090      1049
                             1118                   1067   1082    1100      1063
                             1129                   1081   1093    1102      1073
                             1142         1109      1091        1111   \\V//        1084
                             1150    1133      \\\\\V/////           1115   1106        1097
                        1166 1157    1141 1120                       1123        \\\\\ /////
                        1180 1171    1148 1124                       1130             1114
                        1190 1181    1162 1132                       1135             1121
                        1201 1192    1172 1139                       1145             1126
                             \\V//        1183 1153    1144          1156             1136
                             1205         1196 1163    1154          1169             1147
                        \\\\\\V////////        1174    1165   1177   1186             1160
                             1213         1187 1178    1193   1202        1168
                                   1220        1204    1195     \\\ ///               1184
                                   1225   1234       \\\V//           1207            1198
                                   1235   1244            1211      \\\\\\\\\\\\V/////////
                                   1246   1255            1226                    1217
                                   1259   1268            1237                    1228
                                   1276   1285            1250                    1241
                        1267       1292   1301            1258                    1249
                        1283                \\V//         1274                    1265
                        1297            1306             1288                     1279
                   \\\\\\\\\V//////                       1307                    1298
                             1316               \\\\\\\\\\\\\\\V/////////////
                             1327                         1318
                             1340                         1331
                   1357      1348                         1339
                   1373      1364                         1355
                   1387      1378                         1369
                   1406      1397                 1379    1388
              \\\\\\\\\\V////////                 1399    1408
                        1417 (g)                       \\\V///
                                   1421 (g)
```

110 *Donna Linn*

```
                        1417 (f)                                                    g
                          1430          1421 (f)
                          1438          1429
                          1454          1445
                          1468          1459
                          1487          1478
                          1507          1498
                             \\\\\\\\ ////////
1469                          1520
1489    1537                  1528
1511    1553                  1544
1519    1567                  1558                          1559
1535    1586                  1577                          1579
1549    1606                  1597          1592            1601
1568       \\\\\\\V/////////              \\\\\\\V//////////
1588          1619                            1690
1610    1627    1636                          1925
1618    1643    1652                          1639
1634    1657    1666                  1649    1658
1648    1676    1685                  1669    1678
1667    1696    1705                  1691    1700
1687       \\\ ///                 1682       \\V//
1729       1718                    1699       1708
1736       1735       1717            \\\\V//////
1742       1751       1733        1724                1715
1756       1765       1747        1738                1729
1775       1784       1766        1757        1739    1748
1795       1804       1786        1777        1759    1768
   \\\\\ /////        1808        1799        1781    1790                1750
      1817          \\\\\\\\V/////////        1798    1807                1763
      1834            1825        1816          \\V///                    1780
      1850            1841        1832        1823            1805    1796
      1864            1855        1846        1827               \\\V///
      1883            1874        1865        1856               1819
      1903            1894        1885        1876               1838
         \\\\\\\\\\\\\\\V/////////            1907               1876
                      1916            \\\\\\\V//////            1838
                      1933            1924        1906          1880
                      1949            1940              \\\\\\\\V//////
                      1972            1954                    1922
                      1991            1973                    1936
                      2011            1993                    1955
              \\\\\\\\\\\\\\\\\\\V////////////////            1975
                          2015                                1997
                   \\\\\\\\\\\\\\\\\\\\\V///////////////////////////
                                2023 (i)
```

Breaking the Code 111

```
                                                                                    h
1021
1025
1033
1040
1045    1054
1055    1064
1066    1075
1079    1088
1096    1105
   \\V//
   1112
   1117
   1127
   1138
   1151
   1159
   1175
   1189
   1208    1199
     \\\\\V/////
       1219
       1232                              1210
       1240         1256         1223    1214
       1247         1270         1231    1222
       1261         1280         1238    1229
       1271    1300    1291      1252    1243
       1282         \\V//         1262    1253
       1295         1304         1273    1264                    1289
         \\\\\\\V///////          1286    1277                    1309
           1312                   1303    1294        1313        1322
           1319                    \\V//               1321        1330
           1333         1324       1310               1328        1337
           1343         1334       1315               1342        1351
           1354         1345       1325               1352        1361
           1367         1358       1336               1363        1372
           1384         1375       1349               1376        1385
           1400         1391       1366               1393        1402
             \\\\\V/////            1382                \\\\\\\V/////////
              1405                  1396                    1409
                \\\\\\\\\\\\\V/////////////     1414        1423
                        1415                    1424        1433
                        1426                    1435        1444
                        1439                    1448        1457
              1447      1456                    1465        1474
              1463      1472                    1481        1490
              1477      1486                    1495        1504
              1496      1505                      \\\\\\\V/////////
                \\\\\\\V/////////                    1514
                        1516                         1525
                        1529                         1538
                        1546                         1555
                        1562                         1571
                        1576                         1585
                        1595                         1604
                  \\\\\\\\\\\\\\\\\\\\\V//////////////////////
                                    1615 (i)
```

112 *Donna Linn*

```
1513                                                                                    i
1523
1534
1547
1564
1580
1594            1603
   \\\\\\\\V////////
        1613
        1624            1615 (h)
        1637            1628
        1654            1645
        1670            1661
        1684            1675
        1703            1694
            \\\\\\\\V////////
                1714
                1727
                1744
                1760
1783            1774
1802            1793
   \\\\\\\\V////////
        1813
        1826
        1843
        1859                            1772
        1882            1873            1789
        1901            1892            1814
            \\\\\\\\V////////            1828
                1912                    1847
                1925            1867    1829
                1942            1889    1849
                1958            1915    1871    1910 (j)
1963            1984            1931    1888    1921
1982            2000            1945    1913    1934
   \\\\\\\\V////////            1964    1927    1951
        2002                    1984    1946    1967
            \\\\\\\\\\\V////////////    1966    1990
                2006                    1988    2009
                    \\\\\\\\\\V////////////    2020
2023 (g)        1996            2014            2024
2023                \\\\\\\\V////////            2023
2035                    2021                    2039
2045                    2026                    2053    2044
2056                    2036                    2063    2054
2069                    2047                    2074    2065
2086            2077    2060                    2087    2078
2102            2093    2068                    2104    2095
   \\\\\\\\V////////    2084                        \\V//
        2107            2098                        2111 (k)
            \\\\\\\\V////////
                2117  (k)
```

Breaking the Code 113

```
1345                                                                                              j
1360
1370
1381            1390
1394            1403                    1412
      \\\\\\V///////                    1420
        1411            1436            1427
        1418            1450            1441
        1432            1460            1451
        1442            1471            1462
        1453            1484            1475    1480
        1456            1501            1492    1493            1502
        1483                   \\\\\\\V////////        \\\\\\\\\V////////
        1499                    1508                    1510            1526
            \\\\\\\\\\\V////////////                    1517            1540
                        1522                            1531            1550
                        1532                            1541    1570    1561
                        1543                            1552    1583    1574
                        1556                            1565    1600    1591
                        1573                            1582        \\V//
                        1589                            1598            1607
                        1612                                \\\\\V////////           1616
                        1622                                    1621                 1630
                        1633                                    1631                 1640
                        1646                                    1642    1660         1651
                        1663                                    1665    1673         1664
                        1679                                    1672    1690         1681
                1693    1702                                    1688    1706         1697
                  \\\\\V////////                                    1711        \\\\\\\V////////
                        1712                                    1721            1720
                        1723                                    1732            1730
                        1736                                    1745            1741
                        1753                                    1762            1754
                        1769                                    1778            1771
                        1792                                    1801            1787
                            \\\\\\\\\\\\\\\\\\V/////////////////////////////       1810
                                    1811                                        1820
                                    1822                                        1831
                                    1835                                        1844
                                    1852                                        1861
                                    1868                                        1877
                                    1891                                        1900
                                        \\\\\\\\\\\\\\\\\\\\\V//////////////////////////
                                            1910   (i)
```

114 *Donna Linn*

```
1919                                                              k
1939
1961
1978
2003            1985
       \\\\\\\\\V/////////
        2008
        2018
        2029
        2042
        2050            2033
        2057   2066    2041
        2071   2080    2048
        2081   2090    2062
        2092   2101    2072
           \\V//       2083
            2105       2096
               \\\\V/////
                2113
                2130
2134            2125
2144            2136
2155            2146
2168            2159                                    2117 (i)   2111 (i)
2185            2176                                    2128       2116
2201            2192       2176                         2141       2126
   \\\\\\V//////          2183                          2149       2137
      2206                2197                          2165       2150
         \\\\\\\\\V///////////                          2179       2158
                 2216                                   2198       2174
                 2227          2246                        \\\V/////  2188
2257....         2240          2260                        2218       2207
2273             2264          2281                        2231
2287             2278  2290    2294                        2239
2306             2297  2303    2311                        2255
    \\\\\\\V/////////    \\\\\\\\V/////////                2269
                 2317           2318      2279            2288
                 2330           2332      2299            2308
                 2338           2342        \\\\\\\\V/////////
                 2354           2353            2321
                 2368           2366            2345
                    \\\\\\\\\\\\\\\V//////////////////  2359
                           2387                 2378
                           2407                 2398
                               \\\\\\\\\\\\\\\\V////////////////////
                                        2420
                                        2428    2437
                                        2444    2453
                                        2458    2467
                                        2477    2486
                                        2497    2506
                                          \\\\\\\\V/////////
                                            2519
                                            2536   2527 (l)
```

Breaking the Code 115

```
2369                                                                                          |
2389                                                         2459
2411                                                         2479
2419                                              2492       2501
2435                                                   \\\\\\\\\V///////
2449                                                   2509
2468   2519                                            2525
2510   2536            2527 (k)                        2539
2518   2552            2543                            2558
2534   2566            2557                  2549     2578
2548   2585            2576                  2569     2591
2567   2605                         2596     2591     2600
2587       \\\\\\\\V////////        2582            \\V///
2609          2618                  2599         2608
2626          2635                     \\\\\\\\\V////////////   2617
2642          2651                  2624                        2633
2656          2665                  2638                        2647
2675          2684                  2638                        1647
2695          2704                  2657                        2666
    \\\\\\\\\V////////              2699                        2708
         2717                              \\\\\\\\\\\\\V/////////////
         2734                              2725
         2750                              2741
         2764                              2755
         2783                              2774
         2803                              2794
    \\\\\\\\\\\\\\\\\\\\V///////////////////////////////
                   2816
                   2833
                   2849
                   2872
                   2891        2900
                       \\\\\\\V/////////
                        2911 (n)
```

116 *Donna Linn*

```
1840            1862                                                    m
1853            1872
1870    1895    1904
2886       \\\\\\\V/////////
1909            1918
1928            1937
1948            1957
1970            1979
1987            2005    1952    1930
   \\\\\\\\V/////////    1969    1943
        2012            1994    1960
           \\\\\\\V/////////    1976
                2017            1999
                   \\\\\\\\V/////////
                    2027
                    2038
                    2051
                    2059
                    2075
                    2089
        2099        2108
           \\\\\\\V/////////
                2119
                2132
                2140        2156        2123    2110
                2147        2170        2131    2114
                2161        2180        2138    2122
                2171    2200    2191    2152    2129
                2182        \\V//       2162    2143
                2195    2204            2173    2153
                   \\\V//////           2186    2164    2189
                        2212            2203    2177    2209
                        2219                    2194    2222        2213
        2224    2233                \\\\\\\V/////////   2230        2221
        2234    2243                    2210            2237        2228
        2245    2254                    2215            2251        2242
        2258    2267                    2225            2261        2252
        2275    2284                    2236            2272        2263
        2291    2300                    2249            2285        2276
           \\\V//////                   2266            2302        2293
                2305                    2282               \\\\\\\\\V/////////
       \\\\\\\\\\\\\\\\\\\V/////////////////////   2296        2309
                        2315            2314            2323
                        2326            2324            2333
                        2339            2335            2344
        2347            2346            2348            2357
        2363            2372            2365            2374
        2377            2386            2381            2390
        2396            2405            2395            2404
           \\\\\\\V/////////                        \\\\\\\\V/////////
                2416  (n)                           2414  (n)
                                                    2425
```

Breaking the Code 117

```
2413                                                        n
2423                              2414 (l)
2434              2416  (l)       2425
2447              2429            2438
2464              2446            2455
2480              2462            2471
2494   2503       2476            2485
   \\V//          2495            2504
   2513              \\\\\\\V////////
   2524              2515
   2537              2528
   2554              2545
   2570              2561
   2584              2575
   2603              2594
      \\\\\\\\\\\\\\V////////////////
              2614
              2627
              2644
              2660
2683          2674
2702          2693
   \\\\\\\V////////
       2713
       2726
       2743
       2759
2773   2782
2792   2801
  \\V//
  2812
  2825
  2842
  2885
  2881                              2918
  2900       2891                   2938
     \\\\\V//////     2920    2942  2960
 (l) 2911             2933    2959  2977
     2924             2950    2984  3002
     2941             2966      \\V//
     2957             2989      3007                          2975
     2980             \\\\\\\V////////    3016                2998
     2999                 3017                  \\\\\\\V////////
        \\\\\\\\\\\\\V////////////           3026
                 3028                        3037
                 3041                        3050
                 3049                        3058
                 3065                        3074
                 3079                        3088
                 3098                        3107
            \\\\\\\\\\\\\\\\\\\\\\\\V//////////////////////////////
                           3118  (p)
```

118 *Donna Linn*

```
2312                                                                              o
2320
2327        2336
2341        2350
2351        2360
2362        2371
2375        2384                                              2380
2392        2401                              2402            2393
   \\\\\\\V///////   2383                        \\\\\\\V///////
        2408         2399      2426         2410
    \\\\\\\V///////            2440         2417
             2422             2450         2431
             2432    2470     2461         2441
             2443    2483     2474         2452
             2356    2500     2491         2485
             2473        \\\\\\\\\\V/////  2482
             2489          2507            2498
             2512     \\\\\\\\\\\\\V/////////           2516
             2522            2521                      2530
             2533            2531                      2540
             2546            2542      2560            2551
             2536            2555      2573            2564
             2579            2572      2590            2581
2593         2602            2588      2606            2597
   \\\\\\\V///////                        \\\\\\\V///////
        2612                 2611                2620
        2623                 2621                2630
        2636                 2632                2641
        2653                 2645                2654
        2669                 2662                2671
        2691                 2678                2687
         \\\\\\\\\\\\\\\\V/////////////////   2700
                  2711                              2720
                  2722                              2731
                  2735                              2744
                  2752                              2761
                  2768                              2777
        2819      2791                              2800
        2839          \\\\\\\\\\\\\\\\V/////////////////
        2861     2852        2810
        2878     2869        2821
        2903     2894        2834
         \\\\\\\V///////     2851
             2917            2867
             2936            2890        2909
             2956                \\\\\\\V///////
             2978                    2929
             3004    2986            2951
              \\\\\\\V///////        2968
                  3011               2993
                 \\\\\\\\\\\\\\\\V/////////////////
                          3016  (n)
```

Breaking the Code 119

```
                    2650                                                                    p
                    2663
                    2680
      2672    2696          2705
      2689          \\\\\\\V///////
      2714          2719
      2728          2738
      2747          2758
      2767          2780                  2729
      2789          2797        2806      2749
      2815          \\\\\\\\\V/////////   2771    2740
      2831               2822             2788    2753
      2845               2836             2813    2770
      2864               2855             2827    2786
      2884               2875             2846    2809
      2906               2897             2866    2828
           \\\\\\\\\\\\\V////////////     2888    2848    2830
                 2923                     2914    2870    2843
                 2939                     2930    2887    2860
                 2962                     2944    2912    2876           2885
                 2981                     2963    2929    2899           2908
                 3001                     2983    2945          \\\\\\\V/////////
              \\\\\\\\\\\\\\\\\V//////////////////  2965          2927
                       3005                         2987          2947
                   \\\\\\\\\\\\V////////////                       2969
                          3013                                    2995
                        ////////////////////////////////
                                    3020
                          3034      3025
                          3044      3035
                          3055      3046
                          3068      3059
                          3085      3078
                          3101      3092            3067
                     \\\\\\\\\V/////////             3083
                          3106                      3097
                          \\\\\\\\\\\V////////////
                                    3116
      3118    (n)                   3127
      3131                          3141
      3139              3157        3148
      3155              3173        3164
      3169              3187        3178
      3188    3179      3206        3197
      3208    3199            \\\\\\\\\V/////////
         \\\\\\\V/////////          3217
                 3221               3230
                 3229               3238
                 3245               3254
                 3259               3268
                 3278               3287
                 3298               3307
                  \\\\\\\\\\\\\V////////////
                          3320  (r)
```

120 *Donna Linn*

```
2615                                                                    q
2629
2648    2639
2668    2659
2690    2681
2707    2698
    \\V/         2716
   2723         2732
   2737         2746
   2756         2765
   2776         2785
   2798         2807
      \\\V/////              2762
       2824                  2779
       2840        2795      2804
2863   2854          \\\\\\V/////////
2882   2873             2818
2902   2893             2837
   \V/                  2857
  2915                  2879
  2923           2896   2905
  2948              \\V//
  2971         2953     2921
  2990         2972     2935
  3010         2992     2954         3008
    \\\\\V//////        2974         3019
        3014            2996         3032
         \\\\\\\\\V///////////   3023  3040  3056
                3022             3031  3047  3070
                3029             3038  3061  3080
                3043             3052  3071  3091  3100
                3053             3062  3082     \\V//
                3064             3073  3095     3104                3089
                3077             3086    \\\\\V////                 3109
                3094             3103         3112       3113       3122
                 \\\\\\\\\\V///////////       3119       3121       3130
                        3110           3124   3133       3128       3137
                        3115           3134   3143       3142       3151
                        3125           3145   3154       3152       3161
                        3136           3158   3167       3163       3172
                        3149           3175   3184       3176       3185
                        3166           3191   3200       3193       3202
                        3182             \V//               \\\\\\\V////////
                        3196            3205               3209
                         \\\\\\\\\\\V///////////////   3214       3223
                                3215                   3224       3233
                                3226                   3235       3244
                                3239                   3248       3257
                3247            3256                   3265       3274
                3263            3272                   3281       3290
                3277            3286                   3295       3304
                3296            3305                      \\\\\\\V////////
                 \\\\\\\V////////                         3314 (r)
                        3316 (r)
```

Breaking the Code 121

```
                        3313                                                        r
              (q)       3323
      (q)     3314      3334            3269                    3320    (p)
     3316     3325      3347            3289          3337      3328
     3346     3355      3364            3311          3353      3344
     3362     3371      3380            3319          3367      3358
     3376     3385      3394    3403    3335          3386      3377            3359
     3395     3404      \\\V///         3349          3406      3337            3379
              \\V//             3413    3368          \\\\\\\V/////////  3392   3401
              3415              3424    3388                  3419      \\V//
              3428              3437    3410    3427          3436      3409
              3445              3454    3418    3443          3452      3425
              3461              3470    3434    3457          3466      3439
              3475              3484    3448    3476          3485      3458    3449
              3494              3503    3467    3496          3505      3478    3469
              \\\\\\\V/////////         3487    \\\\\\\V/////////       3500    3491
              3514                      3509          3518      3482    \\\V//
              3527                      3526          3535      3499            3508
              3544                      3542          3551      3517    \\\\\\\V/////////
              3560                      3556          3566      3533    3524
              3574     3583             3575          3584      3547    3538
              3593     3602             3596          3604      3566    3557
              \\V/                      \\\\\\V/////////         3586   3577
              3613                      3617                    3608    3599
              3626                      3626                    \\\\\\\V/////////
              3643                      3634                    3625
              3659                      3650                    3641
     3673     3682                      3664                    3655
     3692     3701                      3683                    3674
     \V////                              3703                   3694
              3712                      \\\\\\\\\\\\\V///////////////////
              3725                              3716
              3742                              3733
              3758                              3749
              3781                              3772
              3800                              3791
              \\\\\\\\\\\\\\\V////////////////////////////
                               3811
                               3824
                               3841
                               3867
                               3880
              3908             3899
              \\\\\\\V/////////
                       3928
                       3950
                       3967
                       3992
                       4015
```

122 *Donna Linn*

New stems

```
3146
3160
3170
3181    3190
3194    3203    3212
        \\\V//  3220
        3211    3227    3236
        3218    3241    3250
        3232    3251    3260
        3242    3262    3271
        3253    3275    3284            3280
        3266    3292    3301    3302    3293
        3283            \\V//           \\V//
        3299            3308            3310            3326
            \\\\\V//////////            3317            3340
                    3322                3331            3350
                    3332                3341            3361    3370
                    3343                3352            3374    3383
                    3356                3365            3391    3400
                    3373                3382                    \\\V//
                    3389                3398                    3407
                    3412                    \\\\\\V/////////            3416
                    3422                    3421                        3430
                    3433                    3431                        3440
                    3446                    3442                        3451    3460
                    3463                    3455                        3464    3473
                    3479                    3472                        3481    3490
                    3502            3493    3488                        3497            3506
                        \\\\\\V/////////    3511                            \\\\\\V/////////
                            3512            3521                                3520
                            3523            3532                                3530
                            3536            3545                                3541
                            3553            3562                                3554
                            3569            3578                                3571
                            3592            3601                                3587
                                \\\\\\\V/////////////                            3610
                                    3611                                        3620
                                    3622                                        3631
                                    3635                                        3644
                                    3652                                        3661
                                    3668                                        3677
                                    3691                                        3700
                                        \\\\\\\\\\\\\\\V////////////////////////////////
                                                        3710
```

Breaking the Code 123

```
New stem                                    3515                                                    t
3710                                        3529
3721                                        3548        3539
3734                                        3568        3559
3751                                        3590        3581
3767                                        3607        3598
3790                                            \\\\\\\V///////      3616
3809           3818                                 3623        3632
3829           3838                                 3637        3648
3851           3860       3820                      3656        3665
3868           3877       3833                      3676        3685
3893           3902       3850                      3698        3707
    \\\\\\\\V////////    3866                           \\\\\\V////////
           3916          3889                               3724
           3935          3917                               3740
           3955          3937                               3754        3763
           3977          3959                               3777        3782
           4003          3985                               3793        3802
              \\\\\\\\\\V/////////////                          \\\\\\V////////
                       4010                                       3815
                                                                  3832
                                                                  3848
                                                                  3871
3550                                                              3890
3563                                                              3910
3580                                                              3923
3596    3605         3572                                         3940
  \\V////             3589                                        3956
   3619               3614                                        3979
   3638               3628                                        4007
   3658               3647
   3680               3667
   3697     3706      3689      3640
     \\\\\V//////      3715     3653
           3722        3731     3670
           3736        3745     3686    3719
           3755        3764     3709    3739                                  3730
           3775        3794     3728    3761       3752                       3745
           3797        3806     3748    3778       3769                       3760
              \\\\\\\V////////  3770    3803       3794    3785               3776
                      3823      3787      \\\\\\\V///////  3808               3799
                      3839      3812         3817                \\\\\\V////////
              3853    3862      3826         3836                    3827
              3872    3881      3845         3856                    3847
              3892    3901      3865         3878                    3869
                \\\V//          3887         3904                    3895
                3914            3913            \\\\\\\\\\V/////////////
                3931            3929                3920
                3947            3952                3934
                3947            3971                3953
                3970            3991                3973
                3989            4013                3995
                4018               \\\\\\\\\\\\\\\V////////////
                                                4021
```

124 *Donna Linn*

New stems   u
3998   3842   3932   3919
4027   3859   3949   3941   3976
            3884   3875   3974   3958   3976
            3907   3898   3997   3983   4001
                \\\\\\\\V////////   4025   \\\\\\\\V////////   3965
                    3926   4006   3988
                    3946   \\\\\\\\V////////
                    3968   4016
                    3994
                    4019

3629   3662
3649   3679
3671   3704   3695
3688   \\\\\\\\V////////
3713   3718
3727   3737
3746   3757
3766   3779
3788   3805   3796
3814   \\\\\\\\V////////
3830   3821
3844   3835
3863   3854
3883   3874
3905   3896
    \\\\\\\\\\\\\\V//////////////
            3922
            3938   3886
            3961   3943   3911
            3980   3962   3925
            4000   3982   3944
                \\\\\\\\V////////   3964
                    4004   3986
                        \\\\\\\\\\\\V////////////
                                4012

Breaking the Code 125

Here is a pattern of numbers within the thousands different again from the nines and the three/sixes. We see a spiral of similar numbers within each of the thousands of years. The one-year entry stems are consistent with five exceptions (in 53 stems) from the year 197 to 3809.

The single years that bring two stems together are as follows:

101-103-107	200	206	208	305
		1106	1108	1205
		See below	2008no	2105
				3005-3013

307	404	406	505	608	707	808
1207	1304	1306	1405	1508	1607	1708
2107	2204	2206	2305	2408	2507	2608
3007-3016	3104	3106	3205	3308	3407	3508

At the change of centuries, we again have single years bringing two stems together twice.

101-103-107	202-206	1012-1016
1003-1007-1015	2002-2006-2014	2012-2017
2007-3017	3005-3013	3011-3016

New stems--one year entry:

97			
	1109		
299	1199	2099	
400	1300	2200	3100
602	1502	2402	3302
692	1592	2492	3392
703	1603	2503	3403
793	1693	2593	3493
905	1905	2705	3605
995	1895	2795	3695
	1906	2806	3706
	1985		2885 part of 2s; 3785 part of 2s
	1996	2896	3796
		2891	
		2909	

2+7   2+7+3   1+7+4   7+2

Two year stems
86-100

187-203	277-293	479-499	490-503
1087-1103	1177-1193	1379-1399	1390-1403
	2077-2093	2279-2299	2290-2303
		3179-3199	3190-3203

580-593	782-799	883-902	973-992
1480-1493	1682-1699	1783-1802	1873-1892
2380-2393	2582-2599	2683-2702	2773-2792
3280-3293	3482-3499	3583-3602	3673-3682

1963-1982	2885-2908	2975-2998	3965-3988
2863part of 3s	3785-3808	3875-3898	
3763part of 3s			

Three year stems:

176-190-200
1076-1090-1100-1102

367-383-397	659-679-701	670-683-700
1267-1283-1297	1559-1579-1601	1570-1583-1600
2167-2183-2197	2459-2479-2501	2470-2483-2500
3067-3083-3097	3359-3379-3401	3370-3383—3400

749-769-791	962-679-1004	1952-1969-1994
1649-1669-1691	1862-1879-1894	2852-2869-2894
2549-2569-2591	2762-2779-2804	3752-3769-3794
3449-3469-3491	3662-3679-3704	

| 2863-2882-2902 | 2942-2959-2984 |
| 3763-3782-3802 | 3842-3859-3884-3907 |

| 2953-2972-2992 | 3943-3962-3982 | 3976-4001-4006 |
| 3853-3872-3892 | | |

Four year stems
64-74-85-98   266-280-290-301   356-370-380-391
                     1166-1180-1190-1201   1256-1270-1280-1291
                     2066-2080-2090-2101   2156-2170-2180-2191
                                               3056-3070-3080-3091

457-473-487-506   547-563-577-596   760-773-790-806
1357-1373-1387-1406   1447-1463-1477-1496   1660-1673-1690-1706
2257-2273-2287-2306   2347-2363-2377-2396   2560-2573-2590-2606
3157-3173-3187-3206   3247-3263-3277-3296   3460-3473-3490-3506

839-859-881-898   850-863-880-896   2942-2959-2984
1739-1759-1781-1798   1750-1763-1780-1796   3842-3859-3884-3907
2639-2659-2681-2698   2650-2663-2680-2696
3539-3559-3581-3598   3550-3563-3580-3596

Begins four and adds five each century

940-953-970-986
1840-1853-1870-1886-1909-1928-1948-1970-1987
2740-2753-2770-2786-2809-2828-2848-2870-2887-2912-2926-2945-2965-2987
3640-3653-3670-3686-3709-3728-3748-3770-3787-3812-3826-3845-3865-3887-3913-
    3929-3952-3971-3991-4013

Five year stems
53-61-68-82-92   154-164-175-188-205
                      1054-1064-1075-1088-1105

244-254-265-278-295   637-653-667-686-706
1144-1154-1165-1178-1195   1537-1553-1567-1586-1606
2044-2054-2065-2078-2095   2437-2453-2467-2486-2506
                                   3337-3353-3367-3386-3406

446-460-470-481-494   727-743-757-776-796
1346-1360-1370-1381-1394   1627-1643-1657-1676-1696
2246-2260-2270-2281-2294-2311   2527-2543-2557-2576-2596
3146-3160-3170-3181-3194   3427-3443-3457-3476-3496

916-932-346-965-985
1816-1832-1846-1865-1885-1907
2716-2732-2746-2765-2785-2807
3616-3632-3646-3665-3685-3707

Start five, add five
929-949-971-988-1013
1829-1949-1871-1888-1913-1927-1946-1966-1988
2729-2749-2771-2788-2813-2827-2846-2866-2888-2914-2930-2944-2963-2983
3629-3649-3671-3688-3713-3727-3746-3768-3788-3714-3830-3844-3863-3883-3876-3905

See also 14 year stems

1930-1943-1960-1976-1999
2830-2843-2860-2876-2899
3730-3743-3760-3776-3799

1919-1939-1961-1976-2003
2819-2839-2861-2878-2903
3719-3739-3761-3778-3803

2918-2938-2960-2977-3002
3818-3838-3960-3877-3902-3985

2920-2933-2950-2966-2989
3820-3833-3850-3866-3889-3917-3937-3959-

Six year stems

143-151-158-172-182-193
1043-1051-1058-1072-1082-1093

334-344-355-368-385-401
1234-1344-1355-1368-1385-1301
2134-2144-2155-2168-2185-2201
3034-3044-3055-3068-3085-3101

424-434-445-458-475-491
1324-1334-1345-1358-1375-1391
2224-2234-2245-2258-2275-2291
3124-3134-3145-3158-3175-3191

536-550-560-571-584-601
1436-1450-1460-1471-1487-1501
2336-2350-2360-2371-2384-2401
3236-3250-3260-3271-3284-3301

626-640-650-661-674-691
1526-1540-1550-1561-1574-1591
2426-2440-2450-2461-2474-2491
3326-3340-3350-3361-3374-3391

815-829-848-868-890-907
1715-1729-1748-1768-1790-1807
2615-2629-2648-2668-2690-2707
3515-3529-3548-3568-3590-3607

817-833-847-866-886-908
1717-1733-1747-1766-1786-1808
2617-2633-2647-2666-2686-2708
3517-3533-3547-3566-3586-3608

1816-1632-1846-1865-1885-1907
2716-2732-2746-2765-2785-2807
3616-3632-3646-3665-3685-3707

3886-3911-3925-3944-3964-3986

Breaking the Code

Seven year stems
233-241-247-262-272-283-296
1133-1141-1147-1162-1172-1183-1196
2033-3041-2047-2062-2072-2083-2096

514-523-535-548-565-581-595
1414-1423-1435-1448-1465-1481-1495
2314-2323-2335-2348-2365-2381-2395
3214-3223-3235-3248-3265-6581-3295

613-623-634-347-664-680-694
1513-1523-1534-1547-1564-1580-1594
2413-2423-2434-2447-2464-2480-2494
3313-3323-3334-3347-3364-3380-3394

716-730-740-751-764-781-797
1616-1630-1640-1651-1664-1681-1697
2516-2530-2540-2551-2564-2581-2597
3416-3430-3440-3451-3464-3481-3497

872-889-914-928-947-967-989
1772-1789-1814-1828-1847-1867-1889-1915-1931-1945-1964-1984
2672-2689-2714-2728-2747-2767-2789-2815-2831-2845-2864-2884-2906
3572-3589-3614-3628-3647-3667-3689-3715-3731-3745-3764-3784-3806

Eight year stems
323-331-338-352-362-373-386-403
1223-1231-1238-1252-1262-1273-1286-1303
2123-2131-2138-2152-2162-2173-2186-2213
3023-3031-3038-3052-3062-3073-3086-3103

413-421-428-442-452-462-472-493
1313-1321-1328-1342-1352-1362-1372-1393
2213-2221-2228-2242-2252-2262-2272-2293
3113-3121-3128-3142-3152-3162-3172-3193

512-520-527—541-551-562-575-592
1412-1420-1427-1441-1451-1462-1475-1492
2312-2320-2327-2341-2351-2362-2375-2392
3212-3220-3327-3241-3251-3262-3275-3292

569-589-611-619-635-649-668-688
1469-1489-1511-1519-1535-1549-1568-1588
2369-2389-2411-2419-2435-2449-2468-2488-2510-2534-2518-2548-2567-2587-2609-2626-2642- 2656-2672-2695
3269-3289-3311-3319-3335-3349-3368-3388-3410-3418-3434-3448-3467-3487-3509-3526-3542-3556-3575-3595

Nine year stems
121-125-133-140-145-155-166-179-196
1021-1025-1033-1040-1045-1055-1066-1079-1096

310-314-322-329-343-353-364-377-394
1210-1214-1222-1229-1243-1253-1264-1277-1294
2110-2124-2122-2129-2143-2153-2164-2177-2194
3010no

940-953-970-986—
1840-1853-1870-1886-1909-1928-1948-1970-1987—
2740-2753-2770-2786-2809-2828-2848-2870-2887-2912-2026-2945-2965-2987—
3640-3653-3670-3686-3709-3728-3748-3770-3787-3812-3826-3845-3865-3887-3913-3929-3952-3971-3991-4013

319-332-340-347-361-371-382-395
3008-3019-3032-3040-3047-3061-3071-3082-3095

3920-3833-3850-3866-3889-3917-3937-3959-3985

Ten year stems
209-220-224-232-239-253-263-274-287-304
1109no
2009no

389-409-422-433-437-451-461-472-485-502
1289-1309-1322-1333-1337-1351-1361-1372-1385-1402
2189-2209-2222-2233-2237-2251-2261-2272-2285-2302
3089-3109-3122-3133-3137-3151-3161-3172-3185-3202

211-215-223-235-245-256-269-286-302-307
1111-1115-1123-1135-1145-1156-1169-1186-1202-1207
2011no

Eleven year stems
7-17-19-29-40-44-52-59-73-83-94

20-22-26-34-41-46-56-67-80-88-104
110-112-116-124-131-136-146-157-170-178-194
1010no

Breaking the Code 131

Twelve year stems
710no
1610-1618-1634-1648-1667-1687-1709-1729-1742-1756-1775-1795
2410no
3410no

872-889-914-928-947-967-989
1772-1789-1814-1828-1847-1867-1889-1915-1931-1945-1964-1984
2672-2689-2714-2728-2747-2767-2789-2815-2831-2845-2864-2884-2906
3572-3589-3614-3628-3647-3667-3689-3715-3731-3745-3764-3784-3806

Thirteen year stems
1-2-4-8-16-23-28-38-49-62-70-77-91

5-10-11-13-17-25-32-37-47-58-71-79-95

Fourteen year stems
2729-2749-2771-2788-2813-2827-2846-2866-2888-2914-2930-2944-2963-2983
3629-3649-3671-3688-3713-3727-3746-3766-3788-3814-3830-3844-3863-3883-3905

2740-2753-2770-3786-2809-2828-2848-2870-2887-2912-2926-2945-2965-2987
3640-3653-3670-3686-3709-3728-3748-3770-3787-3812-3826-3845-3865-3887-3913-3929-3952-3971-3991-4013

Twenty year stem
569-589-611-619-635-649-668-710-718-734-748-767-787-809-826-842-856-875-895
1469-1489-1511-1519-1535-1549-1568-1588-1610-1618-1634-1648-1667-1687-1709-1726-1742-1756-1775-1795
2369-2389-2411-2419-2435-2449-2468-2488-2510-2518-2534-2548-2567-2587-2609-2626-2642-2656-2675-2695
3269-3289-3311-3319-3336-3349-3368-3388-3410-3418-3434-3448-3467-3487-3509-3526-3542-3556-3575-3595

Another way to pattern these numbers is as follows:

1-1000	1000-2000	2000-3000	3000-4000
One stems			
97			
	1109		
299	1199		
400	1300	2200	3100
602	1502	2402	3302
692	1592	2492	3392
703	1603	2503	3403
793	1693	2593	3493
905	1805	2705	3605
995	1895	2795	3695
	1906	2806	3706
	1985		
		2891	
	1996	2896	3796
			3908
		2909	
		2986	
2+7	2+7+3	7+5	7+3
Two stems			
86			
187	1087		
277	1177	2077	
479	1379	2279	3179
490	1399	2290	3190
560			
580	1480	2380	3280
782	1682	2582	3482
883	1783	2683	3583
973	1873	2773	3673
	1963		
		2885	3785
		2975	3875
			3965
			3976
3+7	2+6+1	1+6+2	6+4

Breaking the Code

Three stem

176			
367	1267	2167	3067
659	1559	2459	3359
670	1570	2470	3370
749	1649	2549	3449
962	1862	2762	3562
	1952	2852	3752
		2863	3763
		2942	
		2953	3853
			3943
			3976
1+5	5+1	5+4	5+5

Four stems

64			
	1076		
266	1166	2066	
356	1256	2156	3056
457	1357	2257	3157
547	1447	2347	3247
760	1660	2560	3460
839	1739	2639	3539
850	1750	2650	3550
940			
			3842
			3919
2+6+1	2+6	1+6	6+2

Five stems

53			
154	1054		
244	1144	2044	
446	1346	2246	3146
637	1537	2437	3337
727	1627	2527	3427
916	1816	2716	3616
929			
			3539
			3718
	1919	2819	3719
	1930	2830	3730
		2918	3818
		2920	
			3919
3+4+1	2+4+2	1+4+4	4+6

Six stems

143	1043		
334	1234	2134	3034
424	1324	2224	3124
536	1436	2336	3236
626	1526	2426	3326
815	1715	2615	3515
817	1717	2617	3517
	1816	2716	3616
			3886
1+6	1+6+1	6+1	6+2

Seven stems

233	1133	2033	
514	1414	2314	3214
613	1513	2413	3313
716	1616	2516	3416
872			
5	4	4	3

Breaking the Code 135

Eight stems

319			
323	1223	2123	3023
413	1313	2213	3113
512	1412	2312	3212
569			
5	3	3	3

Nine stems

32			
121	1021		
310	1210	2110	
	1829		
			3008
			3820
	1840		
3	4	1	2

Ten stems

209			
211	1110		
389	1289	2189	3089
3	2	1	1

Eleven stems

7
20
110

3

Thirteen stems

1
5

	1772	2672	3572
2	1	1	1

Fourteen stems

2729
2740

Fifteen stems

3629

Twenty stems

1469   2369   3269
                3640

Chapter 16
DIAMOND OF LIFE

The core of light is the very essence of a person's being. We can put the years of age between each line segment starting at the bottom point and going by nine year intervals up the left side, top point at 54 years, down the right side and ending at the bottom point at 108 years (same point as zero).

The diagrams in this chapter include:

1—core of light

2.—numbers on the diamond

    a. physical area

    b. mental area

    c. emotional area

    d. spiritual area

3—combination core of light and lessons

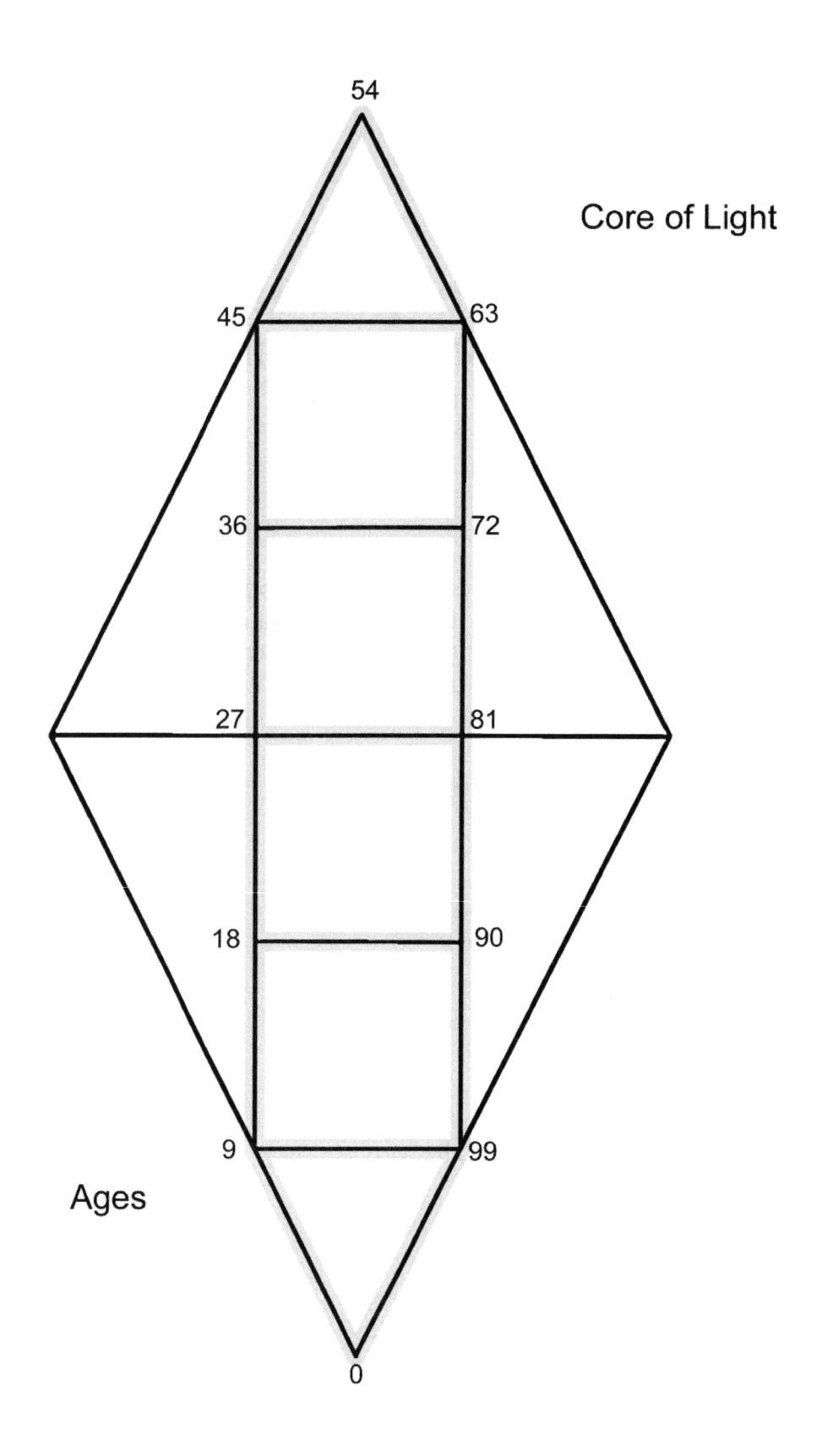

54

Core of Light

45 63

36 72

27 81

18 90

9 99

Ages

0

140 *Donna Linn*

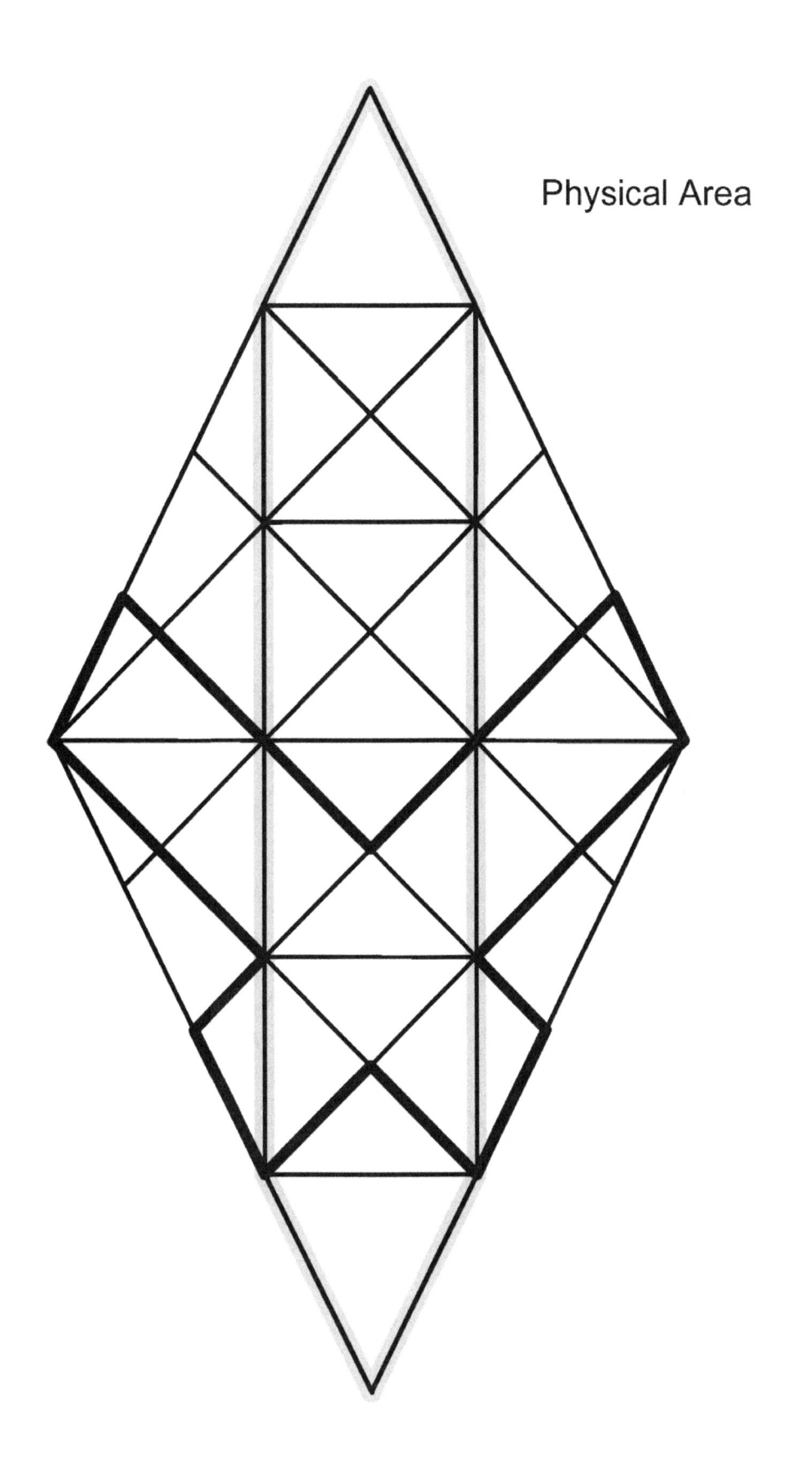

Physical Area

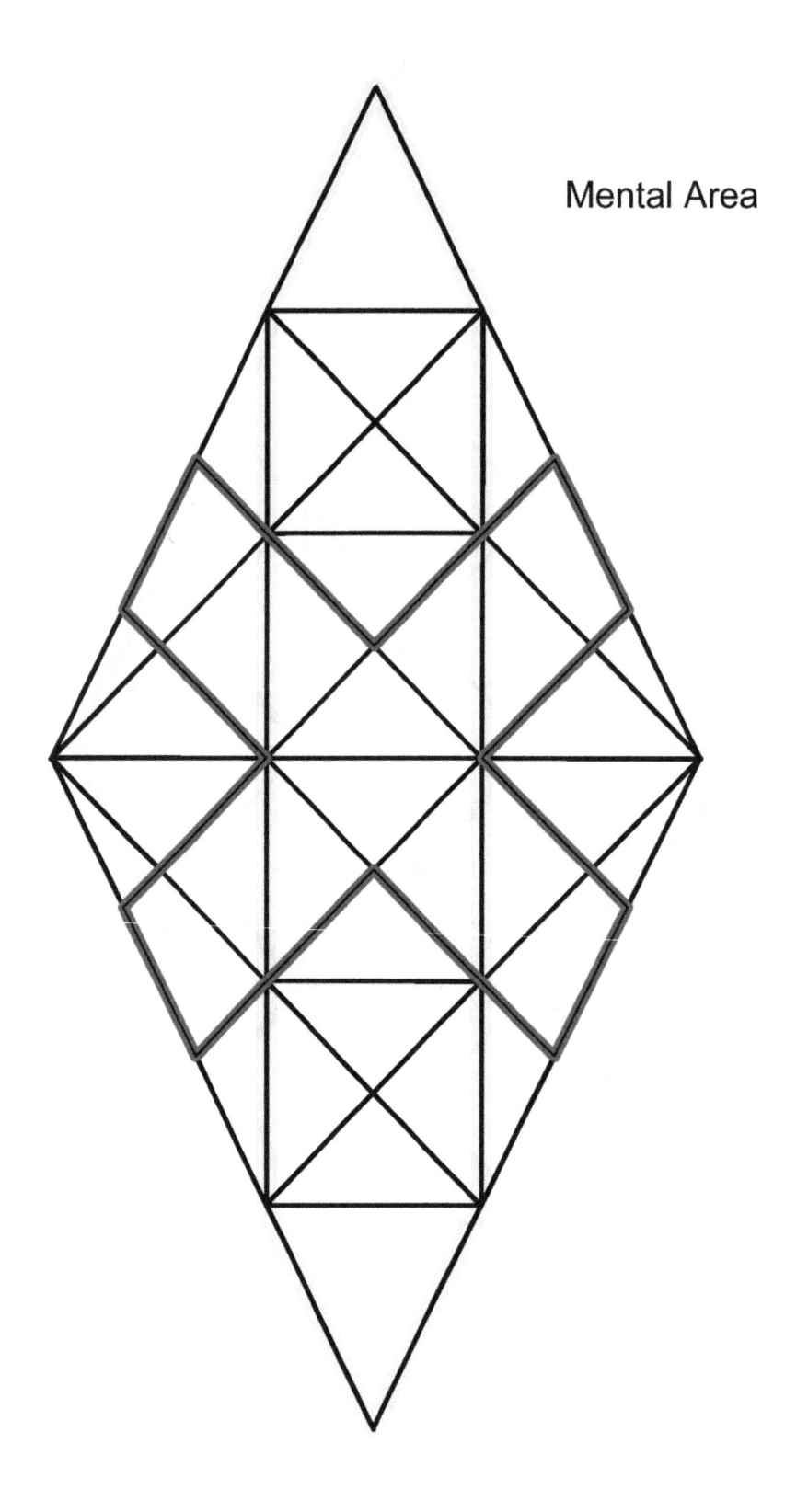

Mental Area

142 *Donna Linn*

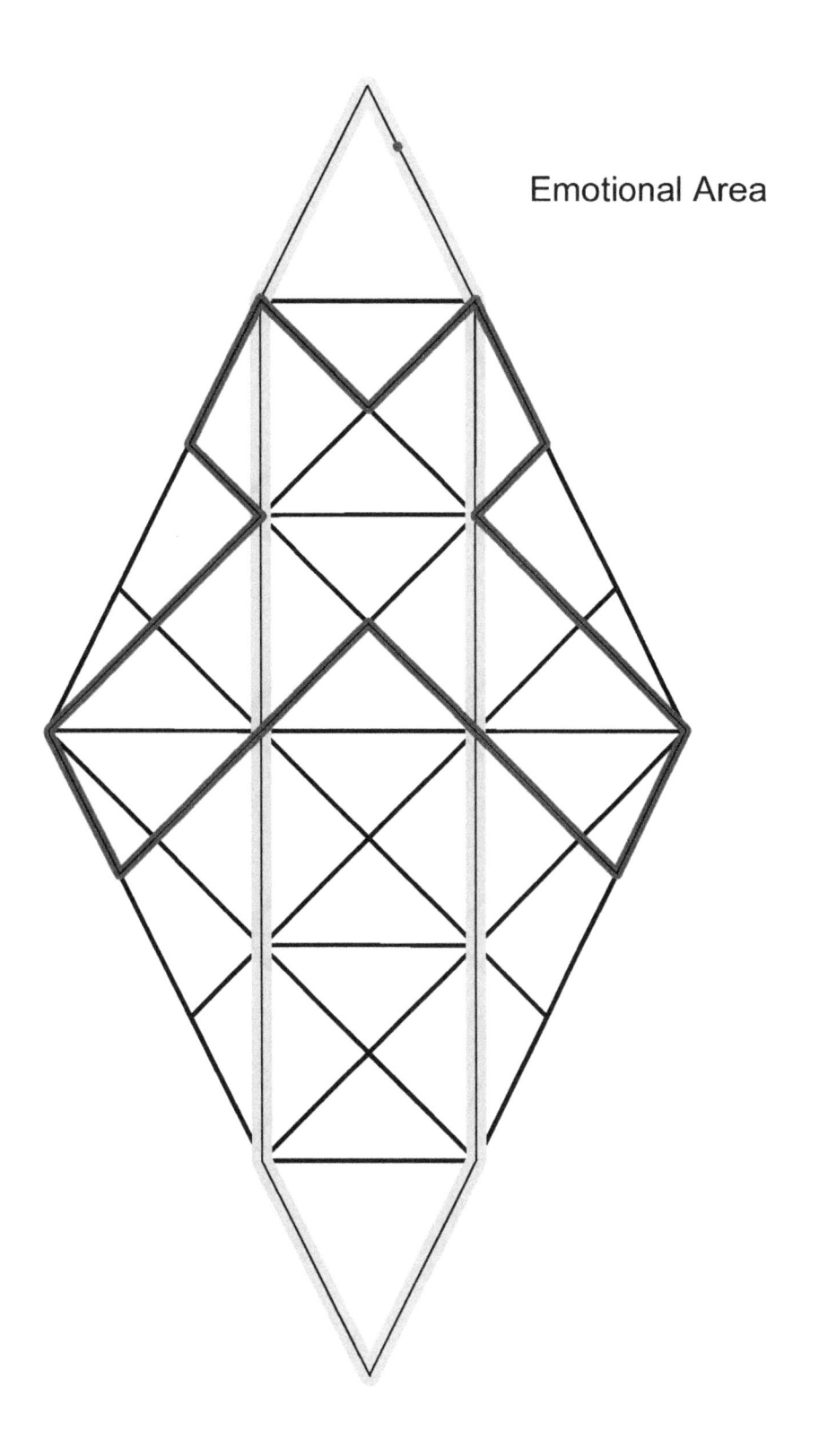

Emotional Area

Breaking the Code 143

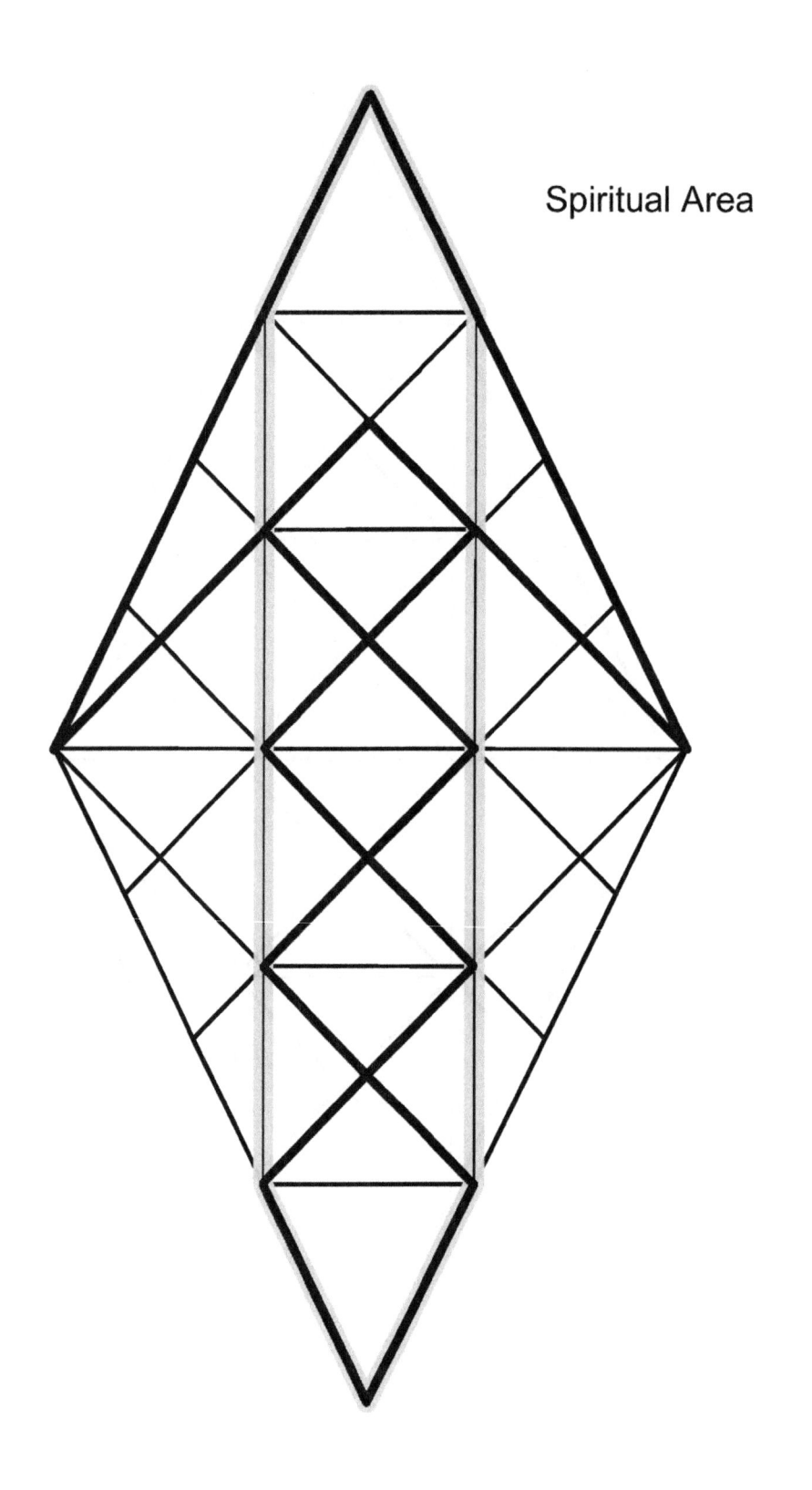

Spiritual Area

144 *Donna Linn*

Combination:
Core of Light
and
Lesson Grid

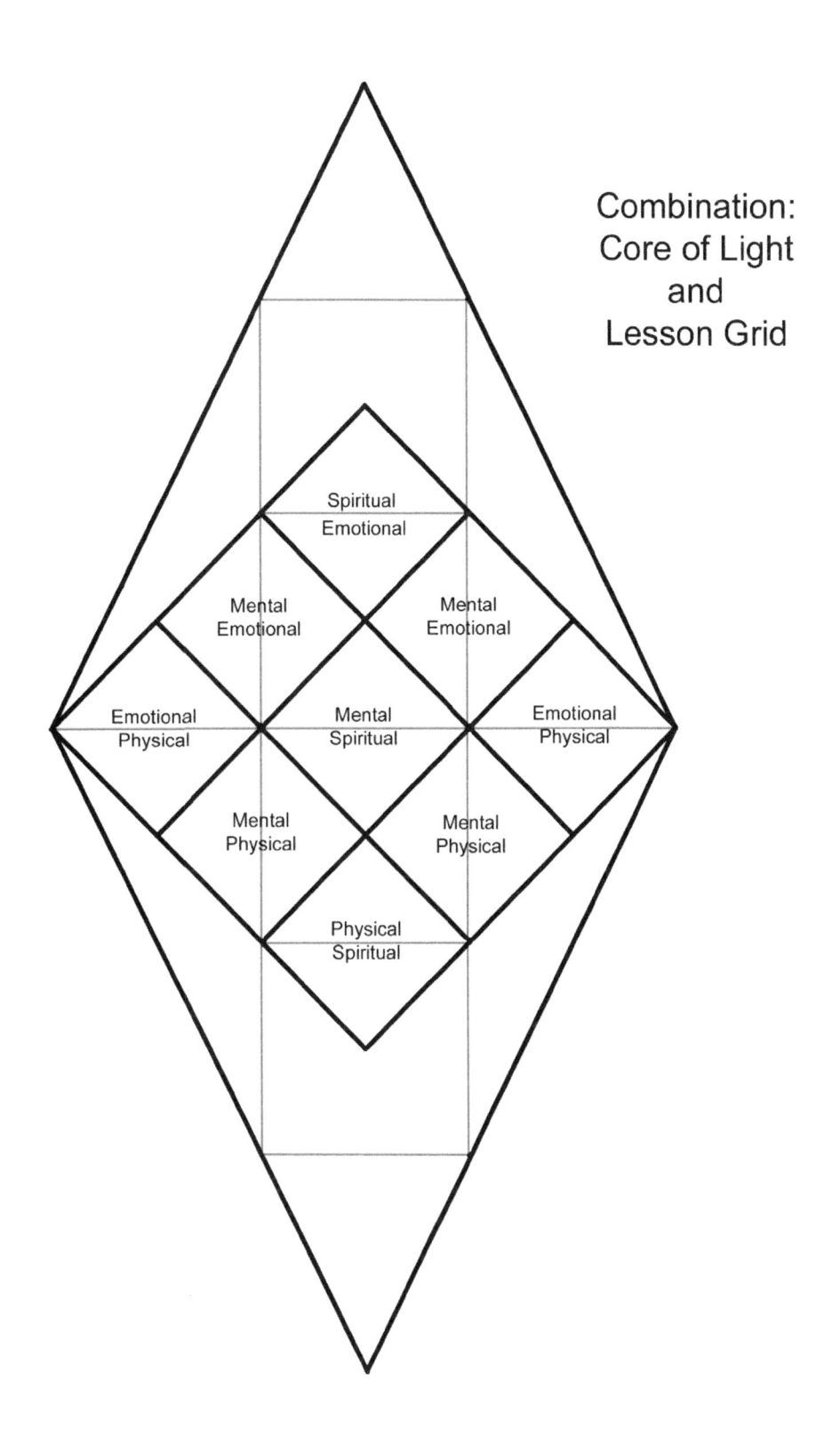

Spiritual
Emotional

Mental
Emotional

Mental
Emotional

Emotional
Physical

Mental
Spiritual

Emotional
Physical

Mental
Physical

Mental
Physical

Physical
Spiritual

Breaking the Code 145

Chapter 17
CONCLUSIONS

There are many things that we don't know about the esoteric numbers and their meanings. Hopefully this will pique an interest in using our 26 letters as numbers instead of only the nine numbers previously utilized as a pathway for learning about ourselves, why we are here, and what we need to learn. It is also a way to wake up those who are sleeping through this incarnation. Numerology is a fascinating tool on the road to understanding where we fit into this marvelous world of creation and is one of the many pathways back to the One.

Much remains to be learned from using the numbers in the expanded form to 26 and perhaps others will also clarify the idea of how the inner and outer numbers work together. The idea of the camera film negative to show the workings of inner numbers toward perfection, as well as a circular ball being pushed from the inside to become perfectly round seems to be the best way for me to describe how these numbers work in our life.

I have worked with these expanded numbers for letters for years now. I am still learning about new patterns and new ways of looking at those numbers.

In summary, this is what I have found and tried to explain in this book.

1. Esoteric numerology is more in depth than exoteric numerology.
2. Esoteric numerology has many more words to describe the numbers than I have given.
3. Esoteric numerology uses master numbers up to 999.
4. Initiation numbers are complement numbers of the master numbers.

5. Initiation complement numbers are either outside-showing numbers of inner master numbers, or inside-showing of outside master numbers.

6. All inner numbers are soul lessons, all outer numbers are physical lessons.

7. There are only 45 physical and 45 spiritual lessons in the first 99 numbers. Looking at these lessons another way, there are 16 physical lessons (14-41), four physical mastery numbers (11-44), nine beginning numbers (1-9), 20 spiritual lessons, and 5 spiritual mastery numbers (55-99).

8. The teen numbers can be either physical or spiritual.

9. Opposite numbers have the same lessons, but different weight—23/32, etc.

10. The higher master numbers 111-999 use only the 3-6-9 reduced numbers. They also divide into physical, physical/spiritual, and spiritual lessons.

11. The higher master number complements use only the 1-4-7 reduced numbers and also have physical, physical/spiritual, or spiritual characteristics.

12. Each civilization has its own lessons to learn.

13. Families seem to come together to work on the same lessons. When one person learns them, then he/she can help the extended family to learn the lesson also.

14. Responsibility for children and decisions made for them lasts until they are of an age to make the decisions for themselves.

15. Using each nine years of age, life can be divided into four parts—childhood, adulthood, maturity, elderly, or into three parts--growth, responsibility and elder knowledge.

16. The years 1-4000 have stems that follow a specific pattern through the century cycles.

17. There are three major groups of numbers in these years: one of nines (and numbers that reduce to nine), one of three/sixes (and numbers that reduce to three and six,) and the rest are 1-2-4-8-7-5 stems (and the numbers that reduce to these numbers).

18. There are ways to find important years in your life—using the date of birth, time and place of birth similar to astrology. Each set of years must be added down, across, and reduced as many times as possible.

19. The diagram of a diamond shows the areas of physical, mental, emotional, and spiritual opportunities for growth. None is better or worse, just different areas.

20. Every person has a center or core of light and the lessons are understood from that perspective.

21. Numerology is just one method of becoming aware of your great purpose in this incarnation, but it is just a tool. Because it is a tool, it can help you navigate better between the lessons to learn—both internally (soul) and externally (physical).

Everyone has a purpose that is meant for that person alone—but if you choose not to accept it the first time, "they" will find another way to help you understand and accept that purpose—but you are always free to reject that purpose. It just means that there will be another time or another place to try again. Numerology helps you discover what lessons both on the physical and on the soul level you came to learn, so if you will, you can take the easier road to these lessons and circumstances in your life

Perhaps someone who reads this book will continue making other parts of this esoteric numerology clear and extending "my" work as I have done from ideas of previous authors. I do not claim to have written this book without help—authors who have written before this for my understanding of basic numerology and that unseen core of Beings who implanted the "what if" as I played with the numbers. Their extended ideas, knowledge, and patterns were the beginnings of this book—I only put them on paper, but I accept responsibility for bringing these ideas to a public forum, so that many other people can use it.

You may find other patterns, have other ideas, gather other knowledge when working with this material. I would welcome more knowledge on the subject of esoteric numerology to come forward into the world.

ADDENDUM

Some other drawings that are not in the book, but are relevant to esoteric numerology are included here for two reasons. One is that they are interesting, and two is that I know that somehow numerology fits into them.

I have written what I know about how the numbers fit into the diamond. There are two ways. One is from one to ninety-nine. The other is from one to 999. The widest part of the diamond is either 55 (1-99) or 99 (1-999). The diagrams show what I think are the lesson numbers, ages, etc. I cannot explain them, but I know they are numerology related!

The diamond shows both sets of numbers on it and divides vertically into areas. The odd numbers are on one side and the even numbers are on the other.

This is somewhat a representation of the Pythagoras number pattern that I first learned in numerology, but the inside is all my discovery. This shows past, present, and future. The infinity symbol connects the personality and soul numbers, the life and destiny numbers, the destiny and power numbers, the psychic self and the center-self numbers.

This diamond shows the center core of life and the numbers which can accommodate lessons physically, mentally, emotionally, and spiritually.

The double terminated crystal has three circles. The top one is for the 2 digit vowel number, the bottom for the 2 digit consonant number, while the middle one consists of the total number of your name. This can be a portal for memories, adventures, and learning. It is the core of life for your life lessons.

This triangle has a double terminated crystal in the middle, with physical, mental, emotional, and spiritual lessons around it. It seems to be the creator core crystal with the lessons folded up around it for this incarnation.

1-99, 1-999

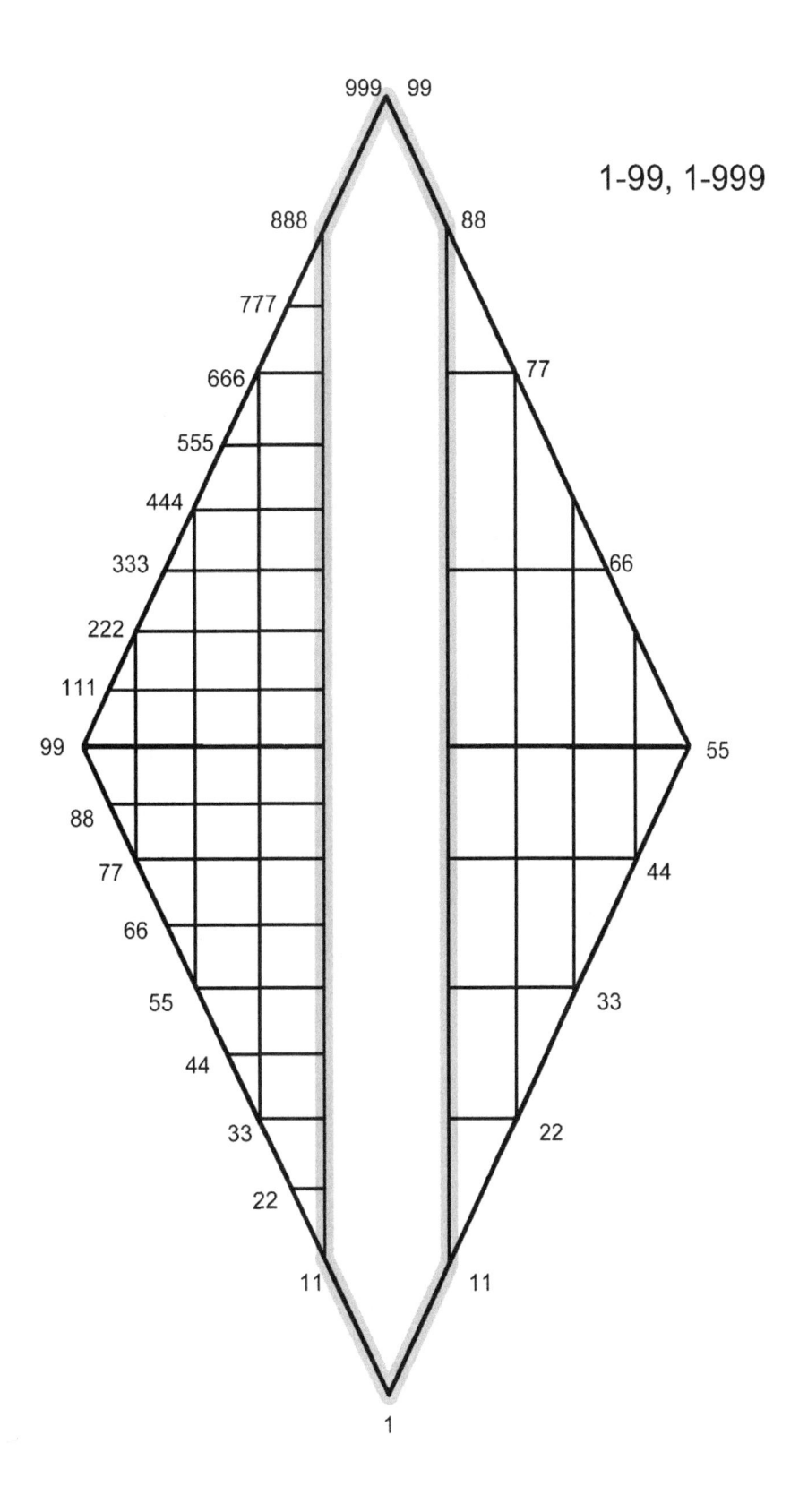

Breaking the Code 153

99
999

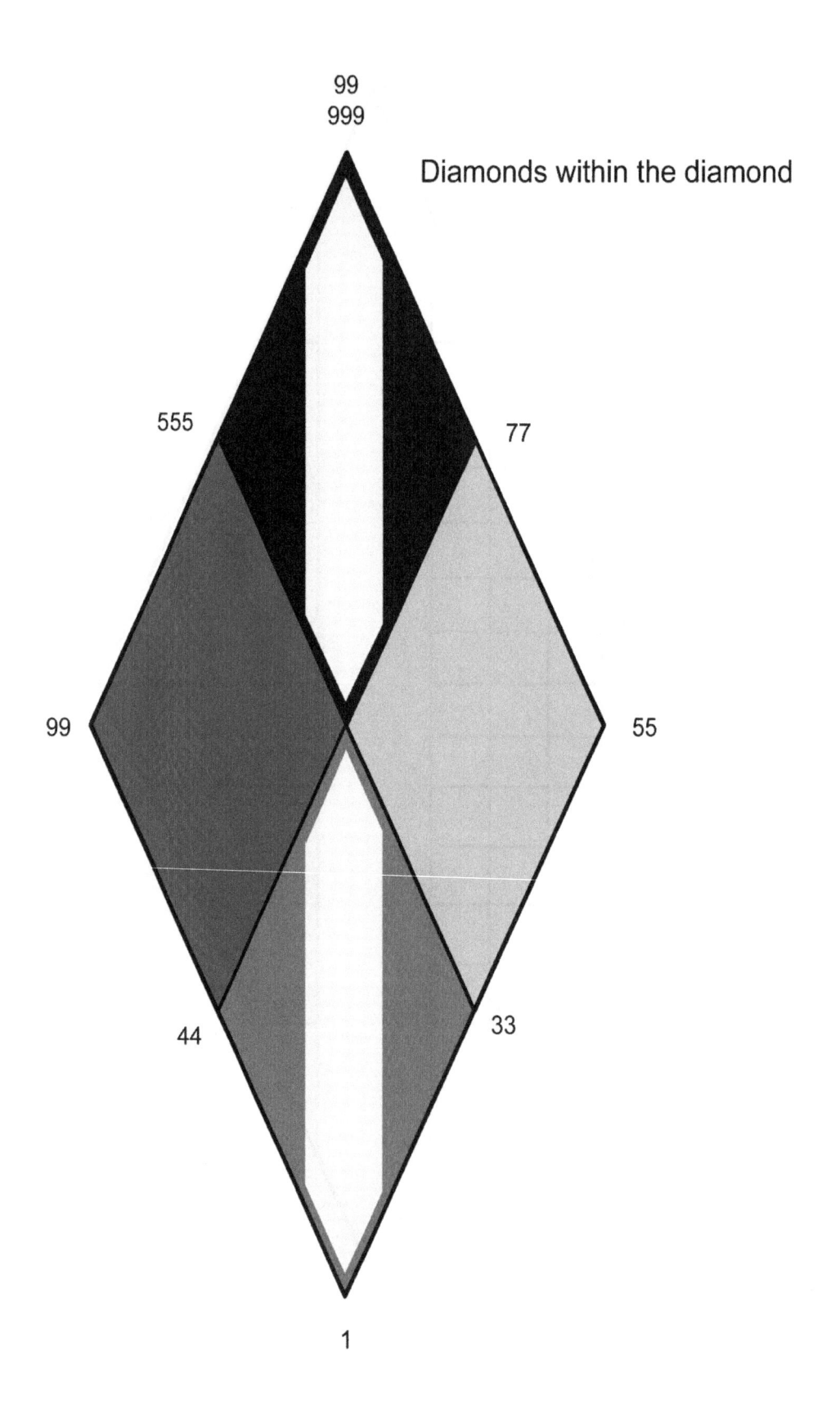

Diamonds within the diamond

555   77

99   55

44   33

1

154 *Donna Linn*

Core of Light with Circles

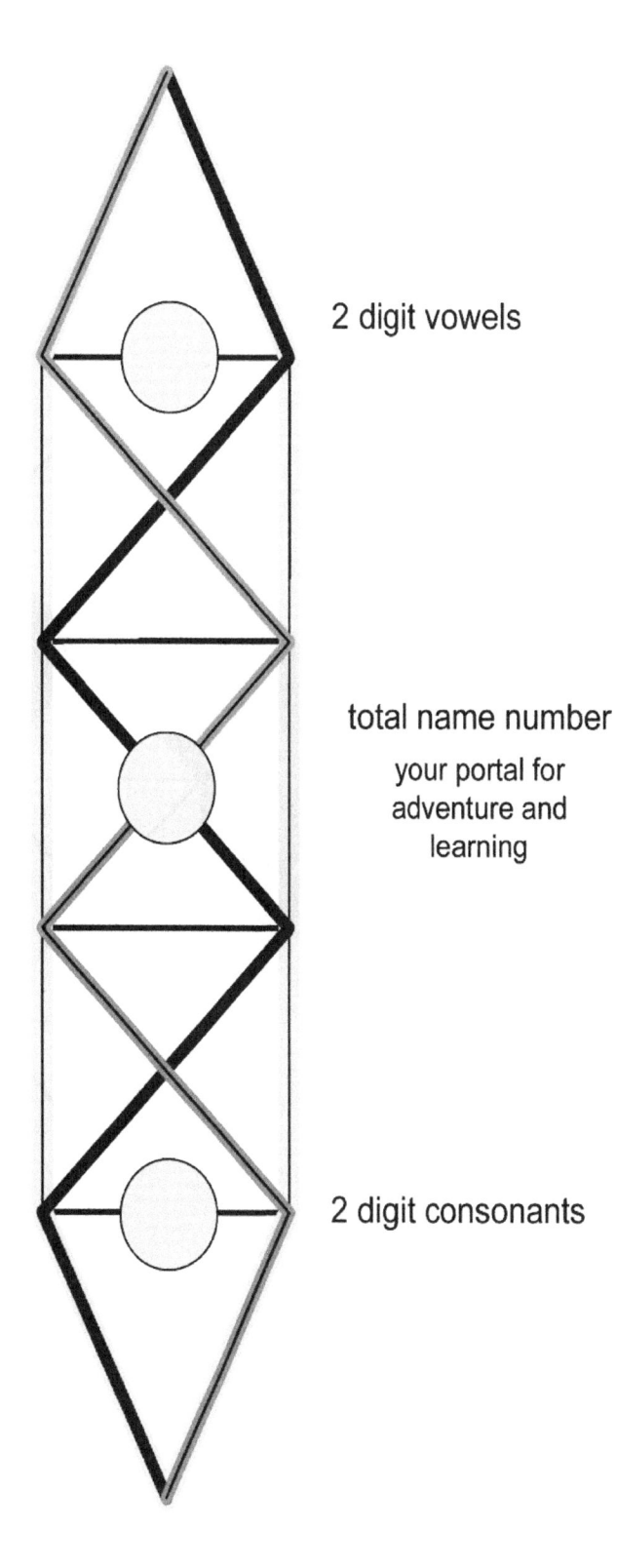

2 digit vowels

total name number
your portal for adventure and learning

2 digit consonants

Breaking the Code

Double terminated crystal with triangle showing lessons with which we come into this incarnation

Past, present, future, with infinity signs

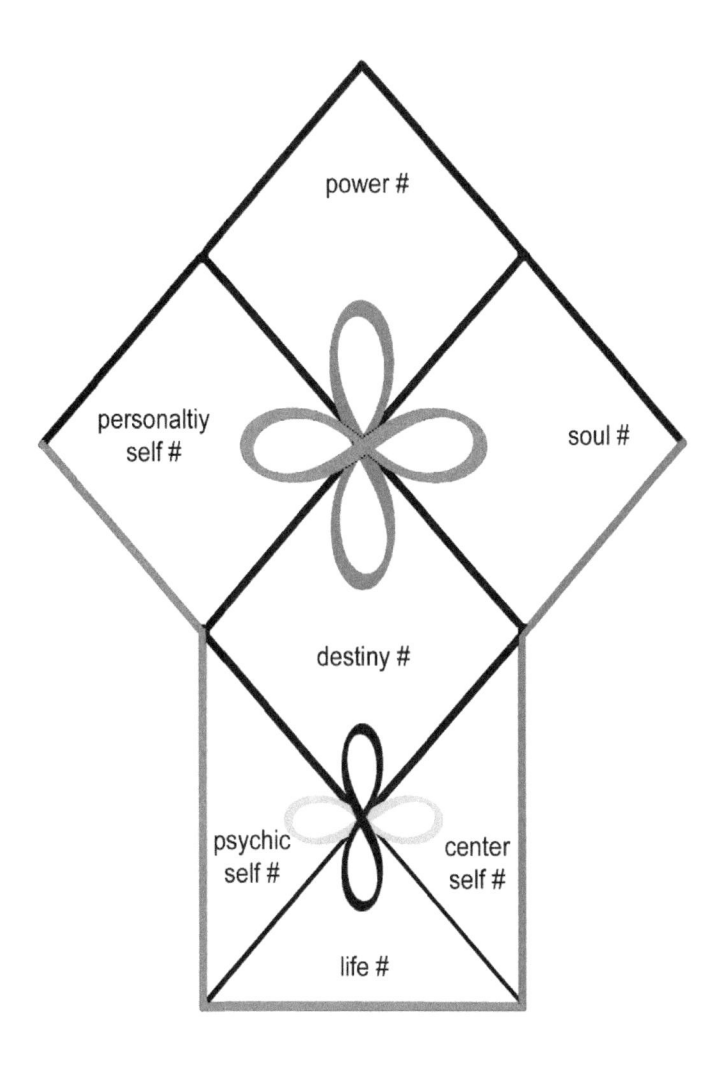

power #

personaltiy self #

soul #

destiny #

psychic self #

center self #

life #

Breaking the Code 157

BIBLIOGRAPHY

Angeli, Annie: THE NUMBERS IN OUR LIVES: A Course in ACP Numerology. AngelLines Publishing, Westport, Connecticut, © 1997

Ashly, Joice: SPIRIT OF NUMEROLOGY. Self published; © revised edn., Oct. 1998

Avery, Kevin Quinn: THE NUMBERS OF LIFE: The Hidden Power in Numerology, rev., enlarged. Dolphin Books, Doubleday and Co., Inc., Garden City, NY, © 1974, 1977

Baillett, Mrs. L. Dow: HOW TO ATTAIN SUCCESS THROUGH THE STRENGTH OF VIBRATION: A System of Numbers as Taught by Pythagoras. Sun Publishing Co., Santa Fe, N. M., © 1905 © 1983

Buess, Lynn M.: NUMEROLOGY FOR THE NEW AGE. DeVorss and Co., Marina del Ray, Ca., © 1978

Bunker, Dusty: NUMEROLOGY AND YOUR FUTURE. Para Research, Rickport, Ma., © 1980

Campbell, Florence: YOUR DAYS ARE NUMBERED: A Manual of Numerology for Everybody. The Gateway, Ferndale, Pa., © 1931, renewed 1958

Cheiro: CHEIRO'S BOOK OF NUMBERS. Arco Publ. Co., New York, N.Y., © 1964

Christy, Albertt: NUMERAL PHILOSOPHY. Publications, Santa Fe N. M., © 1928, © 1981

Connolly, Eileen, THE CONNOLLY BOOK OF NUMBERS: A new path to ancient wisdom. Vol. 1 and 2. Newcastle Publishing Co., Inc., North Hollywood, California, © 1988

David, Karen: NUMEROLOGY ASKS: Who Do You Think You Are Anyway? RKM Publishing Co., Euclid, Oh., © 1982

Claigh, Roberleigh H.: NUMEROLOGY For Personal Transformation: Easy as ABC 123. Gorham Printing, Rochester, Washington, © 1995

Decoz, Hans with Monte, Tom: NUMEROLOGY: Key to Your Inner Self. Avery Publishing Group, Garden City Park, New York, © 1994

Drayer, Ruth: NUMEROLOGY, THE POWER IN NUMBERS: A Right and Left Brain Approach. Jewels of Light Publishing, Mesilla, New Mexico. © 1994

Drayer, Ruth: NUMEROLOGY, The Language of Life. Skidmore-Roth Publishing, El Paso, Texas, © 1990

Gale, Julie: SOUL NUMEROLOGY. Thorsons, an imprint of Harper Collins Publishers, Hammersmith, London, © 1998

Gibson, Walter B.: THE SCIENCE OF NUMEROLOGY. Newcastle Publishinging, Van Nuys, California, © 1995

Goodman, Morris G.: MODERN NUMEROLOGY. Wilshire Book Co., No. Hollywood, Ca., © 1945

Goodwin, Matthew Oliver: NUMEROLOGY, The Complete Guide. Vol. 1 The Personality Reading. Newcastle Publishing Co., Inc., North Hollywood, California, © 1981

Goodwin, Matthew Oliver: NUMEROLOGY, The Complete Guide, Vol. 2 Advanced Personality Analysis and Reading the Past, Present, and Future. Newcastle Publishing Co., Inc., North Hollywood, Ca., © 1981

Gruner, Mark and Brown, Christopher K.: MARK GRUNER'S NUMBERS OF LIFE. Taplinger Publ. Co., New York, N. Y., © 1977

Heline, Corinne: SACRED SCIENCE OF NUMBERS. New Age Press, Inc. LaCanada, Ca., third printing 1976, no copyright.

Javane, Faith: MASTER NUMBERS: Cycles of Divine Order. Whitford Press, A division of Schiffer Publishing, Ltd, Atglen, Pa. © 1988

Javane, Faith and Bunker, Dusty: NUMEROLOGY AND THE DIVINE TRIANGLE. Para Research, Rockport, Massachusetts, © 1972

Johari, Harish: NUMEROLOGY: With Tantra, Ayurveda, and Astrology: A Key to Human Behavior. Destiny Books, Rochester, Vermont, © 1990

Jordan, Juno: MANY THINGS ON NUMEROLOGY. Controversies and Questions. DeVorss and Co., Publ., Marina del Rey, Ca., © 1981

Kozminsky, Isidore: NUMBERS: Their Meaning and Magic. Samuel Weiser, Inc., New York, © 1912, reprinted 1977

Kryder, Rowena Pattee: DESTINY: Gaia Matrix Oracle Numerology. Golden Point, Mount Shasta, California, © 1995

Kurban, Michael J.: NUMEROLOGY PROVEN SOUL SCIENCE. Libra Press, Chicago, Illinois, © 1985

Lawrence, Shirley Blackwell: BEHIND NUMEROLOGY. New Castle Publishing Co., Inc., North Hollywood, California, © 1989

Lawrence, Shirley Blackwell: NUMEROLOGY AND THE ENGLISH CABALAH: Translating Numbers into Words and Words into Numbers. Newcastle Publishing Co., Inc., Van Nuys, California, © 1993

Leek, Sybil: NUMEROLOGY: The Magic of Numbers. Collier Books, The MacMillan Co., Collier-Macmillan, Canada Ltd., Toronto, Ontario, © 1969

Lopez, Vincent: NUMEROLOGY. A Signet Book, New American Library, © 1983

Millman, Dan: THE LIFE YOU WERE BORN TO LIVE: A Guide to Finding Your Life Purpose. H.J. Kramer, Inc., Tiburon, California, © 1993

Moore, Gerun: NUMBERS WILL TELL. Tempo Books, Grossett and Dunlap, New York, N.Y., © 1973

Mykian, W.: NUMEROLOGY MADE EASY. Wilshire Book Co., No. Hollywood, Ca., © 1979

Phillips, Dr. David A.: SECRETS OF THE INNER SELF: The Complete Book of Numerology. Angus and Robertson Publishers, North Ride, Australia, © 1981

Phillips, Ph. D., David A.: THE COMPLETE BOOK OF NUMEROLOGY: Discovering the Inner Self. Hay House, Inc., Carlsbad, California, © 1992

Pitkin, David J. (David James): SPIRITUAL NUMEROLOGY: Caring for Number One. Aurora Publications, Ballston Spa, New York, © 2000

Roquemore, Kathleen: IT'S ALL IN YOUR NUMBERS. Harper and Row, Publ., New York, N. Y., © 1975

Schwaller de Lubicz, R. A.: A STUDY OF NUMBERS: A guide to the Constant Creation of the Universe. Inner Traditions International, Rochester, Vermont, © 1950, first U.S. edition 1986

Schneider, William Alan and Gray, Aline R.: A HANDBOOK FOR NUMEROLOGISTS. Schneider Corporation, Fort Wayne, In., © 1980

Seton, Julia: SYMBOLS OF NUMEROLOGY. Newcastle Publ. Co., Inc., North Hollywood, Ca., © 1984

Shine, Norman: NUMEROLOGY: Your Character and Future Revealed in Numbers. A Fireside Book, Simon & Schuster Inc., New York, © 1994

Stein, Sandra Kovacs: INSTANT NUMEROLOGY: Charting Your Road Map to the Future. Harper Colophon Books, Harper & Row, Publishers, New York, Hagerstown, San Francisco, London, © 1974

Vaughan, Richard: NUMBERS AS SYMBOLS FOR SELF-DISCOVERY. Crcs Publ., Reno, Nev., © 1965

Tanner, Nelda Louise: CHANGING YOUR LIFE WITH NUMBERS: Awareness of Your Potentials. RightLeft Graphics, Chino Valley, AZ, © 1994

Thompson, Leeya Brooke: CHALDEAN NUMEROLOGY: An Ancient Map for Modern Times. Tenacity Press, no city, © 1999

Walton, Roy Page: NAMES, DATES, AND NUMBERS: What They Mean to You. Sun Publishing Co., Santa Fe, N.M., publ. 1981, © 1914,

Webster, Richard: CHINESE NUMEROLOGY: The Way to Prosperity and Fulfillment. Llewellyn Worldwide, St. Paul, MN, © 1998

Westcott, W. Wynn: NUMBERS, THEIR OCCULT POWER AND MYSTIC VIRTUES. Theosophical Publ. House, Ltd., London, Eng., © 1890, 4th edn.1973

Vaughan, Richard: NUMBERS AS SYMBOLS FOR SELF-DISCOVERY. CRCS Publications, Reno, Nev., © 1985

Young, Ellin Dodge: WHAT'S IN A FIRST NAME? EVERYTHING!. Long Shadow Books, Pocket Books, New York, © 1985

ABOUT THE AUTHOR

Donna Linn is available for workshops on this information. Please contact her by email rmes420234@aol.com, or cell phone 859-760-2982.

One workshop teaches you how to use the numbers from 1-26 for a name reading with additional numbers to chart and understand.

The second one teaches how to use your birthdate (and time) to find your (or your client's) important years within the specific physical, mental, emotional, or spiritual areas.

She is also available to teach a new healing method called Galactic Healing using specific nature, angelic and sacred geometry symbols.

Donna is currently working on her second book called **Beyond the Code** due to release in 2012.